DRACULA

DRACULA

The Vampire Play

By Hamilton Deane & John L. Balderston

Adapted from Bram Stoker's Novel,

Dracula

INTRODUCTION BY STANLEY RICHARDS

NELSON DOUBLEDAY, INC.
Garden City, New York

Hamilton Deane—John L. Balderston

In 1897, while the legendary actor, Sir Henry Irving, was stalking the stage of the Lyceum Theatre (London) as the Napoleon to Ellen Terry's *Madame Sans-Gêne* in Sardou's play, the seed of one of the modern theatre's most popular and extensively performed melodramas sprouted, of all places, in the box office of his historic playhouse. That was the year that Sir Henry's devoted business manager-cum-novelist, Bram Stoker, published his fifth novel, *Dracula,* which was destined to become a classic and perhaps the most famous Gothic horror story of all time. Stoker's earlier contributions to literature are all but forgotten, yet *Dracula,* with a tenacity worthy of his vampiric heritage, has managed, through numerous transmogrifications, to survive and "jolt the marrows" of countless millions for almost three quarters of a century.

"Of monsters, famous or infamous," wrote James Nelson in his 1970 preface to the original novel when it was issued in the series of Great Illustrated Classics, "—Cyclops, Dr. Jekyll's Mr. Hyde, the Phantom of the Opera, King Kong, the Hunchback of Notre Dame, Frankenstein's monster—of them all, the one who reigns in enormity is Count Dracula. He was vampire, werewolf, bat, and man."

Admittedly, scarcely a combination of characteristics a guid-

ance counselor would link together as a formula for durable
success. But perhaps the strange hold that Stoker's creation has
exercised undiminishingly through the years can best be
summarized from David Zinman's perceptive commentary in his
book, 50 Classic Motion Pictures: ". . . unlike other monsters,
Dracula is a man who walks among us. And he is more than that.
He is an aristocrat, a titled nobleman . . . He dresses impeccably
and has the cultured good manners and good taste to play the
gracious host to his victims . . . In fact, an irresistible allure per-
vades his entire being. Where other monsters repelled their prey,
Dracula's suave, gallant air, his intense burning eyes, exerted a
hypnotic charm."

Bram (Abraham) Stoker was born in Dublin on November 8,
1847, and like his compatriot, George Bernard Shaw, later "be-
came so prominent in England that most thought him English."
His exceptional diversity propelled his early career in many di-
rections, ranging from journalism to officiating as an Inner Tem-
ple barrister. Most of his later life, however, was given over to
serving as business manager for Sir Henry Irving during the lat-
ter's reign in the English theatre. He remained with Sir Henry
for twenty-seven years, and on occasion, stepped out of the box
office to moonlight as stage manager or even actor when an exi-
gency arose in the company. And, of course, there were his
novels.

Dracula immediately was recognized as a magnificent tale of
horror, "one of the best things in the supernatural line" and "the
very weirdest of weird tales." Though the author published four
more novels before his death in 1912, his immortality is due to a
single literary creation, Dracula.

Years passed before the famed story was adapted for the stage
by Hamilton Deane (1891–1958), son of one of Stoker's child-
hood friends and an accomplished actor who established his own
repertory company and for some twenty years ran seasons in the
English provinces. His dramatization of Dracula had its London
première on February 14, 1927, at the Little Theatre, with
uniformed nurses in attendance to administer to the fainthearted
and the "hopeful staggerers with strained faces queuing up outside the manager's office, putting on some fine performances in

fond hopes of emergency brandy." The play ran for 391 performances, and for more than three years in the provinces, often with Deane in the role of Van Helsing. In 1939, *Dracula* returned to the West End in revival at the Winter Garden Theatre, and later was transferred, either by coincidence or design, to the Lyceum Theatre where it was the penultimate play to occupy the stage on the same site where Stoker once had command of the "front of the house."

A commercial success of such proportions was bound to attract the eye of an American impresario, and in October 1927 *Dracula* was brought to New York by Horace Liveright, a colorfully egocentric publisher who "used his publishing capital to back and produce plays, and his play winnings to back authors." During its transatlantic crossing, *Dracula*, somehow, acquired a collaborator, John L. Balderston, and when the melodrama opened at the Fulton Theatre he shared co-authorship billing with Deane. According to available records, this was a "slightly different version," evidence that also is sustained by a perusal of the disparate London and New York playbills.

John L. Balderston (1889–1954) was an American journalist and foreign correspondent whose variegated career caught the international spotlight in 1926 with the London première of his play *Berkeley Square*, written in collaboration with J. C. Squire. The drama's success was duplicated in New York (1929) with Leslie Howard as star, then as a film for which Mr. Balderston fashioned the screenplay. He wrote several more works for the stage (including his co-authorship of *Dracula*), but most of his subsequent professional life was dedicated to motion picture writing, and among the noted films he contributed to were: *Lives of a Bengal Lancer; Prisoner of Zenda; Smilin' Through; Gone With the Wind;* and *Gaslight*.

At the time of its Broadway opening, the press described *Dracula* as "an evening rich in horror," one that is "blithely blood-curdling" and had the "audience quaking delightedly." The play's engagement lasted for 261 performances, then took to the road where it continued to chill and "jolt" audiences for several more years.

Dracula not only had the very agreeable habit of swelling the coffers of its creators and managements, it catalytically brought lifelong fame to Bela Lugosi, an erstwhile romantic Hungarian actor who essayed the title role on Broadway and later on the screen. Lugosi was the perfect incarnation of Count Dracula, and his masterful performance, even today, is regarded as a classic of cinematic art. His total identification with the part lasted throughout his lifetime and when he died, in 1956, he was buried in Dracula's emblematic black cape. The film's extraordinary popularity signaled an entire new screen trend in vampire epics, though none ever achieved the status or prosperity of the original that emanated from the Stoker novel and the Deane-Balderston play.

Dracula was first presented by Hamilton Deane and H. L. Warburton (by arrangement with Jose G. Levy and Henry Millar) at the Little Theatre, London, on February 14, 1927. It was first produced in the United States at the Fulton Theatre, New York, on October 5, 1927, by Horace Liveright.

The most recent Broadway production of Dracula opened at the Martin Beck Theatre in New York City on October 20, 1977. It was presented by Elizabeth Ireland McCann, John Wulp, Victor Lurie, Nelle Nugent, and Max Weitzenhoffer, and directed by Dennis Rosa. Scenery and costumes were designed by Edward Gorey, and lighting by Roger Morgan. Scenery was supervised by Lynn Pecktal and costumes by John David Ridge. The cast of this production, in order of appearance, was as follows:

LUCY SEWARD	Ann Sachs
MISS WELLS, *maid*	Gretchen Oehler
JONATHAN HARKER	Alan Coates
DR. SEWARD	Dillon Evans
ABRAHAM VAN HELSING	Jerome Dempsey
R. M. RENFIELD	Richard Kavanaugh
BUTTERWORTH	Baxter Harris
COUNT DRACULA	Frank Langella

ACT ONE
  The library in Dr. Seward's Sanatorium, Purley, England.
  Evening.

ACT TWO
  Lucy's boudoir. Evening of the following day.

ACT THREE
  Scene 1: The library. Thirty-two hours later, shortly before
  sunrise.
  Scene 2: A vault. Just after sunrise.

Time
The 1920's

DRACULA

ACT ONE

The library on the ground floor of DR. SEWARD's *Sanatorium at Purley. Room is medieval, the walls are stone with vaulted ceiling supported by two stone pillars, but is comfortably furnished in modern style. Wooden paneling around walls. Tapestries hang on the wall. Medieval fireplace in wall right. Fire burning. There is a divan right center, a large armchair right. At left, a desk with armchair back of it, a small chair to right of desk. Double doors in the rear wall. Large double window across angle of room, left rear, leading out into garden. The curtains are drawn. Door downstage left. Invisible sliding panel in bookcase rear wall right.*

MAID, *an attractive young girl, enters, showing in* JOHN HARKER. HARKER *is a young man of about twenty-five, handsome in appearance; a typical Englishman of the Public School class, but in manner direct, explosive, incisive and excitable.*

HARKER: [*Agitated*] You're sure Miss Lucy is no worse?

MAID: [*Soothingly*] Just the same, sir.

[DR. SEWARD *comes in, downstage left. He is an alienist of about fifty-five, intelligent, but a typical specialist who lives in a world of textbooks and patients, not a man of action or force of character. The* MAID *exits, closing doors*]

SEWARD: Oh! John.

HARKER: [*As* SEWARD *extends hand*] Doctor Seward. What is it? Why have you sent for me?

SEWARD: My dear John. I told you in my wire there was nothing new.

HARKER: You said "no change, don't worry," but to "come at once."

SEWARD: [*Approvingly*] And you lost no time.

HARKER: I jumped in the car and burned up the road from London. Oh, Doctor, surely there must be something *more* we can do for Lucy. I'd give my life gladly if it would save her.

SEWARD: I'm sure you would, my boy. You love her with the warm blood of youth, but don't forget I love my daughter, too. She's all I have. . . . You must see that nothing medical science can suggest has been left undone.

HARKER: [*Bitterly*] Medical science couldn't do much for Mina. Poor Mina.

SEWARD: Yes, poor Mina. She died after these same incredible symptoms that my Lucy has developed.

HARKER: *My* Lucy too.

SEWARD: *Our* Lucy, then.

[*Wild, maniacal laugh is heard offstage left*]

HARKER: Good God, what was that?

SEWARD: [*Sits at desk*] Only Renfield. A patient of mine.

HARKER: But you never keep violent patients here in your sanatorium. Lucy mustn't be compelled to listen to raving madmen.

SEWARD: I quite agree, and I'm going to have him sent away. Until just lately he was always quiet. I'll be sorry to lose him.

HARKER: What!

SEWARD: An unusual case. Zoophagous.

HARKER: What's that?

SEWARD: A life-eating maniac.

HARKER: What?

SEWARD: Yes, he thinks that by absorbing lives he can prolong his own life.

HARKER: Good Lord!

SEWARD: Catches flies and eats them. And by way of change, he feeds flies to spiders. Fattens them up. Then he eats the spiders.

HARKER: Good God, how disgusting. [*Sits*] But tell me about Lucy. [*Leans over desk*] Why did you send for me?

SEWARD: Yesterday I wired to Holland for my old friend Van Helsing. He'll be here soon. The car has gone down to the station for him now. I'm going to turn Lucy's case over to him.

HARKER: Another specialist on anæmia?

SEWARD: No, my boy, whatever this may be, it's not anæmia, and this man, who speaks a dozen languages as well as his own, knows more about mysterious diseases than any one alive.

HARKER: [*Rises*] Heaven knows it's mysterious enough, but surely the symptoms are clear.

SEWARD: So were poor Mina's. Perfectly clear. [*A dog howls at a distance. Other dogs take up the lugubrious chorus far and near.* SEWARD *rises; crosses to fireplace*] There they are, at it again, every dog for a mile around.

HARKER: [*Crosses to window*] They seem howls of terror.

SEWARD: We've heard that chorus every night since Mina fell ill.

HARKER: When I was traveling in Russia, and the dogs in the village barked like that, the natives always said wolves were prowling about.

SEWARD: [*Gets cigarette on mantel; lights it*] I hardly think you'll find wolves prowling around Purley, twenty miles from London.

HARKER: Yet your old house might be in a wilderness. [*Looks out of window*] Nothing in sight except that place Carfax that Count Dracula has taken.

SEWARD: [*Turning from fireplace*] Your friend, the Count, came in again last evening.

HARKER: He's no friend of mine.

SEWARD: Don't say that. He knows that you and I gave our blood for Lucy as well as for Mina, and he's offered to undergo transfusion himself if we need another volunteer. [*Sits on divan*]

HARKER: By Jove, that's sporting of him. I see I've misjudged him.

SEWARD: He seems genuinely interested in Lucy. If he were a young man I'd think . . .

HARKER: What!

SEWARD: But his whole attitude shows that it isn't that. We need sympathy in this house, John, and I'm grateful for it.

HARKER: So am I. Anyone who offers to help Lucy can have anything I've got.

SEWARD: Well, I think he does help Lucy. She always seems cheered up when he comes.

HARKER: That's fine. May I go to Lucy now?

SEWARD: [*Rises*] We'll go together. [*Bell rings off.* HARKER *crosses to door left.* SEWARD *puts out cigarette in ashtray*] That must be Van Helsing. You go ahead and I'll come presently.

[HARKER *exits.* MAID *shows in* ABRAHAM VAN HELSING, *who enters briskly. Man of medium height, in the early fifties, with clean-shaven, astute face, shaggy gray eyebrows and a mass of gray hair which is brushed backward showing a high forehead. Dark, piercing eyes set far apart; nervous, alert manner; an air of resolution, clearly a man of resourceful action. Incisive speech, always to the point; raps his words out sharply and quickly.* VAN HELSING *carries small black bag*]

MAID: Professor Van Helsing.

SEWARD: [*He and* VAN HELSING *shake hands warmly as* MAID *goes out*] My dear Van Helsing, I can never repay you for this.

VAN HELSING: Were it only a patient of yours instead of your daughter, I would have come. You once rendered me a service.

SEWARD: Don't speak of that. You'd have done it for me. [*Starts to ring*] Let me give you something to eat . . . [*Stopped by* VAN HELSING's *gesture*]

VAN HELSING: [*Places bag on table back of divan*] I dined on the boat train. I do not waste time when there is work to do.

SEWARD: Ah, Van Helsing, you cast the old spell on me. I lean on you before you have been two minutes in my house.

VAN HELSING: You wrote of your daughter's symptoms. Tell me more of the other young lady, the one who died.

SEWARD: [*Shows* VAN HELSING *to chair right of desk.* SEWARD *sits at desk*] Poor Mina Weston. She was a girl just Lucy's age. They were inseparable. She was on a visit here when she fell ill. As I wrote you, she just grew weaker, day by day she wasted away. But there were no anæmic symptoms, her blood was normal when analyzed.

VAN HELSING: You said you performed transfusion.

SEWARD: Yes, Sir William Briggs ordered that. [*Baring forearm*] You see this mark? Well, Lucy herself, and her fiancee, John Harker, gave their blood as well.

VAN HELSING: So . . . Three transfusions . . . And the effect?

SEWARD: She rallied after each. The color returned to her cheeks, but the next morning she would be pale and weak again. She complained of *bad dreams*. Ten days ago we found her in a stupor from which nothing could rouse her. She . . . died.

VAN HELSING: And . . . the other symptoms?

SEWARD: None, except those two little marks on the throat that I wrote you about.

VAN HELSING: And which perhaps brought me here so quickly. What were they like?

SEWARD: Just two little white dots with red centers. [VAN HELSING *nods grimly*] We decided she must have run a safety pin through the skin of her throat, trying in her delirium to fasten a scarf or shawl.

VAN HELSING: Perhaps. And your daughter's symptoms are the same?

SEWARD: Precisely. She too speaks of *bad dreams*. Van Helsing, you've lived in the tropics. May this not be something alien to our medical experience in England?

VAN HELSING: [*Grimly*] It may indeed, my friend.

[*Laugh is heard from behind curtain at window.* VAN HELSING *rises, followed by* SEWARD *who crosses to window and draws curtains.* RENFIELD *is standing there. Repulsive youth, face distorted, shifty eyes, tousled hair*]

SEWARD: [*Astounded, drawing* RENFIELD *into room*] Renfield. How did you . . . ?

VAN HELSING: Who is this man?

SEWARD: [*Crosses to bell; rings*] One of my patients. This is gross carelessness.

VAN HELSING: Did you hear us talking?

RENFIELD: Words . . . words . . . words . . .

SEWARD: Come, come, Renfield, you know you mustn't wander about this way. How did you get out of your room?

RENFIELD: [*Laughs*] Wouldn't you like to know?

SEWARD: How are the flies? [*To* VAN HELSING] Mr. Renfield makes a hobby of eating flies. I'm afraid you eat spiders, too, sometimes. Don't you, Renfield?

RENFIELD: Will you walk into my parlor, said the spider to the fly. Excuse me, Doctor, you have not introduced me to your friend.

SEWARD: [*Reprovingly*] Come, come, Renfield.

VAN HELSING: Humor him.

[*Enter* MAID]

SEWARD: Tell the Attendant to come here at once.

MAID: Yes, sir. [*Exits*]

SEWARD: Oh, very well. Professor Van Helsing, Mr. Renfield, a patient of mine.

[VAN HELSING *steps toward him. They shake hands.* VAN HELSING *rubs* RENFIELD's *fingers with his thumb and* RENFIELD *jerks hand away*]

RENFIELD: Ah, who does not know of Van Helsing! Your work, sir, in investigating certain obscure diseases, not altogether unconnected with forces and powers that the ignorant herd do not believe exist, has won you a position that posterity will recognize.

[*Enter* ATTENDANT *dressed in uniform. He starts at seeing* RENFIELD *then looks at* SEWARD *sheepishly*]

SEWARD: [*As severely as his mild nature permits*] Butterworth, you have let your patient leave his room again.

ATTENDANT: Blimme, sir, I locked the door on 'im, and I've got the key in my pocket now.

SEWARD: But this is the second time. Only last night you let him escape and he tried to break into Count Dracula's house across the grounds.

ATTENDANT: 'E didn't get out the door this time, sir, and it's a drop of thirty feet out of the windows. [*Crosses to* RENFIELD]

He's just a bloomin' eel. Now you come with me. [*As they start toward door; holds* RENFIELD *by coat collar and right arm*]

SEWARD: Renfield, if this happens again you will get no more sugar to spread out for your flies.

RENFIELD: [*Drawing himself up*] What do I care for flies . . . now? [ATTENDANT *gives* VAN HELSING *a look*] Flies. Flies are but poor things. [*As he speaks he follows with his eyes a fly.* ATTENDANT *sees fly too; releases* RENFIELD *indulgently. With a sweep of his hand he catches fly, holds closed hand to ear as if listening to buzz of fly as he crosses a few steps, then carries it to his mouth. Then seeing them watching him, releases it quickly*] A low form of life. Beneath my notice. I don't care a pin about flies.

ATTENDANT: Oh, doncher? Any more o' yer tricks and I'll take yer new spider away.

RENFIELD: [*Babbles; on knees*] Oh, no, no! Please, dear Mr. Butterworth, please leave me my spider. He's getting so nice and fat. When he's had another dozen flies he'll be just right, just right. [*Gives little laugh. Rubs hands together, then catches fly and makes gesture of eating*]

VAN HELSING: Come, Mr. Renfield, what makes you want to eat flies?

RENFIELD: [*Rises*] The wings of a fly, my dear sir, typify the aerial powers of the psychic faculties.

SEWARD: [*To* ATTENDANT *wearily*] Butterworth, take him away.

VAN HELSING: One moment, my friend. [*To* RENFIELD] And the spiders?

RENFIELD: [*Impressively*] Professor Van Helsing, can you tell me why that one great spider lived for centuries in the tower of the old Spanish church—and grew and grew? He never ate, but he drank, and he *drank*. He would come down and drink the oil of all the church lamps.

SEWARD: [*To* ATTENDANT] Butterworth.

RENFIELD: One moment, Doctor Seward . . . [VAN HELSING *gets wolfsbane from bag on table*] I want you to send me away, now, *tonight,* in a straight waistcoat. Chain me so I can't escape. This is a sanatorium, not a lunatic asylum. This is no place for me. My cries will disturb Miss Lucy, who is ill. They will give your daughter *bad dreams,* Doctor Seward, *bad dreams.*

SEWARD: [*Soothingly*] We'll see about all this in the morning. [*Nods to* ATTENDANT, *who moves toward* RENFIELD]

VAN HELSING: Why are you so anxious to go?

RENFIELD: [*Crosses to* VAN HELSING; *hesitates, then with gesture of decision*] I'll tell *you.* Not that fool Seward. He wouldn't understand. But you . . . [*A large bat dashes against window.* RENFIELD *turns to the window, holds out his hands and gibbers*] No, no, no, I wasn't going to say anything . . .

[ATTENDANT *crosses up; watches* RENFIELD]

SEWARD: What was that?

RENFIELD: [*Looks out window, then turns*] It was a bat, gentlemen. Only a bat! Do you know that in some islands of the Eastern seas there are bats which hang on trees all night? And when the heat is stifling and sailors sleep on the deck in those harbors, in the morning *they* are found dead men . . . white, even as Miss Mina was.

SEWARD: What do you know of Miss Mina? [*Pause*] Take him to his room!

VAN HELSING: [*To* SEWARD] Please! [*To* RENFIELD] Why are you so anxious to be moved from here?

RENFIELD: To save my soul.

VAN HELSING: Yes?

RENFIELD: Oh, you'll get nothing more out of me than that. And I'm not sure I hadn't rather stay . . . After all, what is my soul good for? Is not . . . [*Turns to window*] . . . *what I am to receive worth* the loss of my soul?

SEWARD: [*Lightly*] What's got him thinking about souls? Have you the souls of those flies and spiders on your conscience?

RENFIELD: [*Puts fingers in his ears, shuts eyes, distorts face*] I forbid you to plague me about souls! I don't want their *souls.* All I want is their life. The blood is the life . . .

VAN HELSING: So?

RENFIELD: That's in the Bible. What use are souls to me? [*To* VAN HELSING] I couldn't eat them or dr . . . [*Breaks off suddenly*]

VAN HELSING: Or drink . . . [*Holding wolfsbane under his nose,* RENFIELD's *face becomes convulsed with rage and loathing. He leaps back*]

RENFIELD: You know too much to live, Van Helsing! [*He suddenly lunges at* VAN HELSING. SEWARD *and* ATTENDANT *shout at the attack and as they drag* RENFIELD *to door he stops struggling and says clearly:*]

RENFIELD: I'll go quietly. [SEWARD *lets go of him*] I warned you to send me away. Doctor Seward, if you don't you must answer for my soul before the judgment seat of God!

[RENFIELD *and* ATTENDANT *exit. Wild laughter can be heard off.* VAN HELSING *puts wolfsbane in bag as* SEWARD *closes door*]

SEWARD: My friend, you're not hurt?

VAN HELSING: No.

SEWARD: My deepest apologies. You'll think my place shockingly managed . . .

[VAN HELSING *waves apology aside with impatient gesture*]

What was your herb that excited him so?

VAN HELSING: Wolfsbane. [*A little look out of window as he crosses*]

SEWARD: Wolfsbane? What's that? I thought I knew all the drugs in the pharmacopoeia

VAN HELSING: One of the . . . eremophytes. Pliny the Elder mentions the plant. It grows only in the wilds of Central Russia.

SEWARD: But why did you bring it with you?

VAN HELSING: It is a form of preventive medicine.

SEWARD: Well, we live and learn. I never heard of it.

VAN HELSING: Seward, I want you to have that lunatic securely watched.

SEWARD: Anything you say, Professor Van Helsing, but it's my Lucy I want you to look after first.

VAN HELSING: I want to keep this man under observation.

SEWARD: [*Annoyed and hurt*] An interesting maniac, no doubt, but surely you'll see my daughter.

VAN HELSING: I must see the records of his case.

SEWARD: But Doctor . . .

VAN HELSING: Do you think I have forgotten why I am here?

SEWARD: [*As they start to go out left*] Forgive me. Of course I'll show you the records, but I don't understand why you're so curious about Renfield, because in your vast experience . . .

[*They exit. The room is empty for a few seconds; then* LUCY *enters, supported by* HARKER. *She is a beautiful girl of twenty, clad in filmy white dressing gown, her face unnaturally pale. She walks with difficulty. Round her throat is wound a scarf. She crosses to desk and leans on it as* HARKER *closes door*]

HARKER: Why, I thought they were here, Lucy.

LUCY: John, do you think this new man will be any better than the others?

HARKER: [*Moving her to divan*] I'm sure he will. Anyway, Lucy, now that I'm back I'm going to stay with you till you get over this thing.

LUCY: [*Delighted*] Oh, John. But can you? Your work in town?

HARKER: [*Seating her, then sitting next to her*] You come first.

LUCY: [*A change comes over her*] I . . . don't think you'd better stay, John. [*A look about room*] Sometimes . . . I feel that I want to be alone.

HARKER: My dear. How can you say that you don't want me with you when you're so ill? You love me, don't you? [*Taking her hand*]

LUCY: [*Affectionately*] Yes, John, with all my soul.

HARKER: Just as soon as you're well enough I'm going to take you away. We'll be married next month. We won't wait till June. We'll stretch that honeymoon month to three months and the house will be ready in July.

LUCY: [*Overjoyed*] John, you think we could?

HARKER: Of course, why not? My mother wanted us to wait, but she'll understand, and I want to get you *away* . . . [*Starts to kiss her. She shudders as he does so*] Why do you shrink when I kiss you? You're so cold, Lucy, always so cold . . . now . . .

LUCY: [*With tenderness but no hint of passion*] Forgive me, dear. I am yours, all yours. [*Clings to him. He embraces her. She sinks back*] Oh, John, I'm so tired . . . so tired.

[SEWARD *and* VAN HELSING *return*]

SEWARD: Lucy dear, this is my old friend, Professor Van Helsing.

[*She sits up; extends her hand to him*]

VAN HELSING: My dear Miss Seward . . . [*He kisses* LUCY's *hand*] you don't remember poor old Van Helsing. I knew you when you were a little girl. So high . . . and now what charm, what beauty. A little pale, yes, but we will bring the roses back to the cheeks.

LUCY: You were so kind to come, Professor.

VAN HELSING: And this, no doubt, is the fortunate young man you are to marry?

SEWARD: Yes, John Harker, Professor.

HARKER: Look here, Professor. I'm not going to get in your way, but if Doctor Seward will have me I'm going to make him give me a bed here until Lucy gets over this thing. [*Turns to* SEWARD] It's absolute hell, being away in London, and of course I can't do any work.

SEWARD: You're most welcome to stay, my boy.

VAN HELSING: Indeed, yes. I should have asked you to stay. I may need you. [*Takes chair from desk to left of divan; turns to* LUCY] Now lie back, so . . . [*Examines her eyelids carefully and feels her pulse*] And now tell me when did this, this weakness first come upon you? [*Sits, after examining eyelids; looks at her gums, examines tips of fingernails, then takes out watch as he feels her pulse*]

LUCY: Two nights after poor Mina was buried I had . . . a bad dream.

VAN HELSING: [*Releases pulse, after looking at watch*] A bad dream? Tell me about it.

LUCY: I remember hearing dogs barking before I went to sleep. The air seemed oppressive. I left the reading lamp lit by my bed, but when the dream came there seemed to come a mist in the room.

VAN HELSING: Was the window open?

LUCY: Yes, I always sleep with my window open.

VAN HELSING: Oh, of course, you're English. [*Laughs*] We Continentals are not so particular about fresh air. And then . . .

LUCY: The mist seemed so thick I could just see the lamp by my bed, a tiny spark in the fog, and then . . . [*Hysterically*] I saw two red eyes staring at me and a livid white face looking down on me out of the mist. It was horrible, horrible!

[HARKER *makes move toward her.* VAN HELSING *stops him by a gesture*]

VAN HELSING: There, there . . . [*Soothingly, taking her hands from her face*] Go on, please.

LUCY: [*Gives little start when* VAN HELSING *touches her hands. Looks at* HARKER *and starts; and at* SEWARD *and starts, then at* VAN HELSING *and relaxes*] The next morning my maid could scarcely wake me. I felt weak and languid. Some part of my life seemed to have gone from me.

VAN HELSING: There have been other such dreams?

LUCY: Nearly every night since then has come the mist . . . the red eyes and that awful face.

[*She puts hands to her face again.* VAN HELSING *soothes her; ad libs, as he takes her hands from face,* "There, there, now."]

SEWARD: We've tried transfusion twice. Each time she recovered her strength.

LUCY: But then would come another dream and now I dread the night. I know it seems absurd, Professor, but please don't laugh at me.

VAN HELSING: I'm not likely to laugh. . . .

[*Gently, without answering, he unwinds scarf from her throat. She puts hand up to stop him and cries,* "No, no." *A look at* HARKER *when her neck is bare. As* VAN HELSING *does so he starts, then quickly opens small black bag on table and returns with microscope; examines two small marks on throat.* LUCY *with eyes closed. Controlling himself with difficulty,* VAN HELSING *puts microscope back in bag, closes it, puts back chair by desk*]

And how long have you had these little marks on your throat?

[SEWARD *and* HARKER *start violently and come to divan. They look at each other in horror*]

LUCY: Since . . . that first morning.

HARKER: Lucy, why didn't you tell us?

SEWARD: Lucy, you've worn that scarf around your throat . . . to hide them!

[LUCY *makes convulsive clutch at throat*]

VAN HELSING: Do not press her. Do not excite her [*To* LUCY] Well?

LUCY: [*Constrained; to* SEWARD *and* HARKER] I was afraid they'd worry you, for I knew that . . . Mina had them.

VAN HELSING: [*With assumed cheerfulness*] Quite right, Miss Lucy, quite right. They're nothing, and old Van Helsing will see that these . . . dreams trouble you no more.

MAID: [*Appears at door*] Count Dracula.

[DRACULA *enters. He is a tall, mysterious man of about fifty. Polished and distinguished. Continental in appearance and manner.* LUCY *registers attraction to* DRACULA]

SEWARD: Ah, good evening, Count.

DRACULA: Gentlemen . . . [*He bows to men; then goes to the divan and bows in courtly fashion*] Miss Seward, how are you? You are looking more yourself this evening.

[LUCY *registers thrill. Alternate moods of attraction and repulsion, unaccountable to herself, affect* LUCY *in* DRACULA'S *presence. But this should be suggested subtly*]

LUCY: [*Quite natural*] I feel better already, Count, now that father's old friend has come to help me.

[DRACULA *turns to* VAN HELSING. LUCY *looks up at* DRACULA, *recoils, and turns to* HARKER]

SEWARD: Count Dracula, Professor Van Helsing.

[*The two men bow*]

DRACULA: A most distinguished scientist, whose name we know even in the wilds of Transylvania. [*To* SEWARD] But I interrupt a consultation.

SEWARD: Not at all, Count. It's good of you to come, and we appreciate your motives.

HARKER: Doctor Seward has just told me of your offer, and I can't thank you enough.

DRACULA: It is nothing. I should be grateful to be permitted to help Miss Lucy in any way.

LUCY: But you do, Count. I look forward to your visits. They seem to make me better.

VAN HELSING: And so I arrive to find a rival in the field.

DRACULA: [*Crosses to* LUCY] You encourage me, Miss Seward, to make them more frequent, as I should like to.

LUCY: [*Looking at him fixedly*] I am always glad to see you.

DRACULA: Ah, but you have been lonely here. And my efforts to amuse you with our old tales will no longer have the same success, now that you have Professor Van Helsing with you, and especially now that Mr. Harker is to remain here.

HARKER: How did you know I was going to stay, Count?

DRACULA: [*Little start*] Can the gallant lover ask such a question? I inferred it, my friend.

HARKER: You're right. Nothing is going to shift me now until Lucy's as fit as a fiddle again.

DRACULA: Nothing?

LUCY: Please come as before, Count, won't you?

[DRACULA *bows to her; kisses her hand.* VAN HELSING *meanwhile has been talking to* MAID]

VAN HELSING: . . . you understand, you will not answer bells. She must not be alone for a single moment under any circumstances, you understand.

[*As* DRACULA *crosses to below desk,* LUCY *leans toward him, extends her hand, then recovers herself.* VAN HELSING *registers that he sees her look at* DRACULA]

MAID: Yes, sir.

VAN HELSING: [*To* LUCY] Good. Your maid will take you to your room. Try to rest for a little, while I talk to your father.

[MAID *comes to divan to get* LUCY. *Pause, as* LUCY *looks at* DRACULA]

SEWARD: Wells, remember, don't leave her alone for a moment.

MAID: Oh, no, sir.

[LUCY *exchanges a long look with* DRACULA *as* MAID *takes her out*]

DRACULA: Professor Van Helsing, so you have come from the land of the tulip, to cure the nervous prostration of this charming girl. I wish you all the success.

VAN HELSING: Thank you, Count.

DRACULA: Do I appear officious, Doctor Seward? I am a lonely man. You are my only neighbors when I am here at Carfax and your trouble has touched me greatly.

SEWARD: Count, I am more grateful for your sympathy than I can say.

VAN HELSING: You, like myself, are a stranger in England, Count?

DRACULA: Yes, but I love England and the great London . . . so different from my own Transylvania, where there are so few people and so little opportunity.

VAN HELSING: Opportunity, Count?

DRACULA: For my investigations, Professor.

SEWARD: I hope you haven't regretted buying that old ruin across there?

DRACULA: Oh, Carfax is not a ruin. The dust was somewhat deep, but we are used to dust in Transylvania.

HARKER: You plan to remain in England, Count?

DRACULA: I think so, my friend. The walls of my castle are broken, and the shadows are many, and I am the last of my race.

HARKER: It's a lonely spot you've chosen . . . Carfax.

DRACULA: It is, and when I hear the dogs howling far and near I think myself back in my Castle Dracula with its broken battlements.

HARKER: Ah, the dogs howl there when there are wolves around, don't they?

DRACULA: They do, my friend. And they howl here as well, although there are no wolves. But you wish to consult the anxious father and the great specialist. . . . May I read a book in the study? I am so anxious to hear what the Professor says . . . and to learn if I can be of any help.

SEWARD: By all means, Count. [DRACULA *bows; exits.* SEWARD *watches him leave. Dogs howl offstage*] Very kind of Dracula, with his damned untimely friendliness, but now what about my daughter?

HARKER: Yes, Professor, what do you think is the matter with Lucy?

VAN HELSING: [*Crosses to window, looks out. Long pause before he speaks*] Your patient, that interesting Renfield, does not like the smell of wolfsbane.

SEWARD: Good heavens. What has that got to do with Lucy?

VAN HELSING: Perhaps nothing.

HARKER: In God's name, Professor, is there anything unnatural or occult about this business?

SEWARD: Occult? Van Helsing! Oh . . .

VAN HELSING: Ah, Seward, let me remind you that the superstitions of today are the scientific facts of tomorrow. Science can now transmute the electron, the basis of all matter, into energy, and what is that but the dematerialization of matter? Yet dematerialization has been known and practiced in India for centuries. In Java I myself have seen things.

SEWARD: My dear old friend, you can't have filled up your fine old brain with Eastern moonshine.

VAN HELSING: Moonshine?

SEWARD: But anyway, come now, what about my daughter?

VAN HELSING: Ah! Seward, if you won't listen to what will be harder to believe than any Eastern moonshine, if you won't forget your textbooks . . . keep an open mind, then, Seward. Your daughter's life may pay for your pig-headedness.

HARKER: Go on, go on, Professor!

SEWARD: I am listening.

VAN HELSING: Then I must ask you to listen calmly to what I am

going to say. Sit down. [VAN HELSING *crosses to window;*
closes curtains. SEWARD *and* HARKER *exchange glances, then*
both look at VAN HELSING *as they sit*] You have both heard the
legends of Central Europe, about the Werewolf, the Vampires?

SEWARD: You mean ghosts, who suck the blood of the living?

VAN HELSING: If you wish to call them ghosts. I call them the undead.

HARKER: [*Quickly*] For God's sake, man, are you suggesting that
Mina, and now Lucy . . .

SEWARD: [*Interrupting*] Of course, I have read these horrible folk
tales of the Middle Ages, Van Helsing, but I know you better
than to suppose . . .

VAN HELSING: [*Interrupting*] That I believe them? I *do* believe
them.

SEWARD: [*Incredulously*] You mean to tell us that vampires actu-
ally exist and . . . and that Mina and Lucy have been attacked
by one?

VAN HELSING: Your English doctors would all laugh at such a
theory. Your police, your public would laugh. [*Impressively*]
The strength of the vampire is that people will not believe in
him.

SEWARD: [*Shaking head*] Is this the help you bring us?

VAN HELSING: [*Much moved*] Do not despise it.

HARKER: [*To* SEWARD] Doctor, this case has stumped all your spe-
cialists. [*To* VAN HELSING] Go on, Professor.

VAN HELSING: Vampires are rare. Nature abhors them, the forces
of good combine to destroy them, but a few of these creatures
have lived on for centuries.

HARKER: [*Excited*] What *is* a vampire?

VAN HELSING: A vampire, my friend, is a man or a woman who is
dead and yet not dead. A thing that lives after its death by
drinking the blood of the living. It must have blood or it dies.
Its power lasts only from sunset to sunrise. During the hours
of the day it must rest in the earth in which it was buried. But,
during the night, it has the power to prey upon the living. [*In-*
credulous move from SEWARD] My friend, you are thinking you
will have to put me amongst your patients?

SEWARD: Van Helsing, I don't know what to think but I confess I simply can't follow you.

HARKER: What makes you think that Lucy has been attacked by such a creature?

VAN HELSING: [*From now on dominating them*] Doctor Seward's written account of these ladies' symptoms at once aroused my suspicion. Anæmia? The blood of three men was forced into the veins of Miss Mina. Yet she died from loss of blood. Where did it go? Had your specialist any answer? The vampire attacks the throat. He leaves two little wounds, white with red centers. [HARKER *rises slowly*] Seward, you wrote me of those two marks on Miss Mina's throat. An accident with a safety pin, you said. So I thought, I suspected, I did not know, but I came on the instant, and what do I find? These same wounds on Miss Lucy's throat. Another safety pin, Doctor Seward?

SEWARD: Do you mean to say that you've built up all this nightmare out of a safety pin? It's true I can't make out why she hid those marks from us.

VAN HELSING: I could tell you that.

SEWARD: [*Pause*] What! I don't believe it. Of course Lucy's trouble can't be *that*.

HARKER: I do believe it. This theory accounts for all the facts that nobody has been able to explain. We'll take her away where this thing can't get at her.

VAN HELSING: She will not want to go.

SEWARD: What!

VAN HELSING: If you force her, the shock may be fatal.

HARKER: But why won't she go if we tell her that her life depends on it?

VAN HELSING: Because the victim of the vampire becomes his creature, linked to him in life and after death.

SEWARD: [*Incredulous, shocked; rises*] Professor, this is too much!

HARKER: Lucy become an unclean thing, a demon?

VAN HELSING: Yes, Harker. *Now* will you help me?

HARKER: Yes, anything. Tell me what to do.

VAN HELSING: It's dangerous work. Our lives are at stake, but so is Miss Lucy's life, so is her soul. We must stamp out this monster.

HARKER: How can we stamp it out now?

VAN HELSING: This undead thing lies helpless by day in the earth or tomb in which it was buried.

SEWARD: A corpse, in a coffin?

VAN HELSING: A corpse, if you like, but a living corpse, sustained by the blood of the living. If we can find its earth home, a stake driven through the heart destroys the vampire. But this is our task. In such a case the police, all the powers of society, are as helpless as the doctors. What bars or chains can hold a creature who can turn into a wolf or a bat?

HARKER: A wolf! Doctor Seward, those dogs howling! I told you they howl that way in Russia when wolves are about. And a bat . . . Renfield said there was a bat.

SEWARD: Well. What of it?

VAN HELSING: [*Reflectively*] Your friend Renfield does not like the smell of wolfsbane.

SEWARD: But what in the world has your wolfsbane to do with all this?

VAN HELSING: A vampire cannot stand the smell of wolfsbane.

HARKER: You suspect that lunatic?

VAN HELSING: I suspect no one and everyone. . . . Tell me, who is this Count Dracula?

SEWARD: Dracula? We really know very little about him.

HARKER: When I was in Transylvania I heard of Castle Dracula. A famous Voivode Dracula who fought the Turks lived there centuries ago.

VAN HELSING: I will make inquiries by telegraph. No, but after all this Thing must be English. Or at least have died here. His lair must be near enough to his house for him to get back there before sunrise. [*To* SEWARD] Oh, my friend, I have only the old beliefs with which to fight this monster that has the strength of twenty men, perhaps the accumulated wisdom and cunning of centuries.

HARKER: This all seems a nightmare. But I'm with you, Professor.

VAN HELSING: And you, Doctor Seward?

SEWARD: It all seems preposterous to me. But everyone else has failed. The case is in your hands at present.

VAN HELSING: [*Sternly*] I need allies, not neutrals.

SEWARD: Very well, then, do what you will.

VAN HELSING: Good. Then bring your daughter here.

SEWARD: What are you going to do?

VAN HELSING: To set a trap. Miss Lucy is the bait.

HARKER: My God, we can't let you do that!

VAN HELSING: There's no other way. I believe this Thing knows that I plan to protect Miss Lucy. This will put it on its guard and the first moment she is alone it will no doubt try to get at her, for a vampire must have blood or its life in death ceases.

HARKER: No, I forbid this.

SEWARD: She's my daughter, and I consent. We'll show the Professor he's mistaken.

HARKER: You allow it only because you don't believe, and I do believe. My God, Doctor, I've heard that lunatic laugh . . . life-eating, you said he was, and you subject Lucy to that risk.

VAN HELSING: [*Interrupting harshly*] I must be master here or I can do nothing! I must know in what form this Thing comes before I can plan how to stamp it out. Bring your daughter here.

[SEWARD *turns and sees* HARKER *looking at him; stares at* HARKER. *There is a short pause, then* HARKER *reluctantly exits.* SEWARD *follows him.* VAN HELSING *thinks a moment, then looks about noting the positions of doors, furniture, etc. He then turns out lights. The room is dark except for the firelight.* VAN HELSING *moves into firelight, looks at divan, then walks back to door and turns, looking at divan, satisfying himself that the light from the fire is sufficient to see anything that happens on the divan. Opens curtains. Suddenly, the double doors open sharply and* VAN HELSING *starts violently; the* ATTENDANT *enters*]

ATTENDANT: Beg pardon, sir. Is Doctor Seward here?

VAN HELSING: What do you want with him?

ATTENDANT: Ole Flycatcher's escaped again, sir.

VAN HELSING: Escaped, how?

ATTENDANT: Gor' blimme, out of the window. The door's still locked and I was in the corridor all the while. It's a drop of

thirty feet to the stone flagging. That loonie's a bloomin' flyin'
squirrel 'e is.

VAN HELSING: [*Commandingly*] Say nothing to Doctor Seward at
present. Nothing, do you hear? Now go.

[ATTENDANT *exits.* VAN HELSING *switches on lights again.*
Enter LUCY, *supported by* HARKER *and* SEWARD]

LUCY: Oh! Oh!

SEWARD: Lucy, you have nothing to fear.

[*They take her to divan*]

VAN HELSING: I want you to lie down here my dear.

LUCY: But Doctor . . .

VAN HELSING: You trust me, do you not? [*She smiles weakly at
him; nods. They place her on divan*] I want you to lie here for
just a little.

LUCY: But . . . I am so frightened.

VAN HELSING: Make your mind passive. Try not to think. Sleep if
you can.

LUCY: I dare not sleep. It is when I sleep . . .

[HARKER *takes her hand*]

VAN HELSING: [*Arranging her on divan head on pillows soothingly*] I know my dear. I know. I am going to cure you with
God's help.

LUCY: Oh, but, Father.

SEWARD: You must do as the Professor says. Come, Harker.

VAN HELSING: Come, Harker.

[VAN HELSING *leads* SEWARD *to the door.* SEWARD *exits.*
HARKER *lingers and* VAN HELSING *calls him.* VAN HELSING
switches off lights as he and HARKER *go out. No movement.*
LUCY *closes her eyes. Low howl is heard outside . . . howl of
a wolf. It is followed by a distant barking of dogs. Firelight
grows dimmer.* DRACULA's *hand appears from back of couch,
then his face.* LUCY *screams; swoons. When* LUCY *screams, ad
libs offstage until* VAN HELSING *switches on lights*]

HARKER: Lucy! Lucy!

SEWARD: Professor, what is it?

[VAN HELSING *enters, followed by* SEWARD *and* HARKER. VAN HELSING *switches on lights. They are just in front of door as a bat flies in the room from window to center, then out of the window*]

VAN HELSING: You saw?

SEWARD: God, what was that?

HARKER: Lucy, Lucy, speak to me!

VAN HELSING: Take her to her room, Harker, quickly.

[HARKER *carries* LUCY *to door as* DRACULA *enters. He looks about, his glance taking in everyone*]

DRACULA: [*mildly, sympathetically*] The patient is better, I hope?

[RENFIELD *gives a wild laugh offstage right.* VAN HELSING, SEWARD *and* HARKER *turn.* RENFIELD *gives a second wild laugh*]

CURTAIN

ACT TWO

LUCY's *boudoir. Window right rear, closed but curtains open. Chairs, small occasional table with toilet articles on it by window. Couch against wall up left center. Mirror on wall. Small stand, with flowers in vase, near couch. Doors, right, leading into bedroom, left, leading into hall. Arch left center.*

The next evening.

Dogs howling. As curtain rises, MAID *enters from bedroom, glances up at window over her left shoulder, takes a few steps, looks back over right shoulder, then to couch and takes newspaper. Sits on couch; reads newspaper. As she turns a page,* ATTENDANT *knocks on hall door.*

MAID: [*Starts*] Who is that?

ATTENDANT: [*Enters; smiles at her*] Excuse me, Miss. Did you 'appen to 'ave seen anything of the Guv'ner's pet looney? 'E's out again, 'e is.

MAID: [*Holding paper*] And what would he be doing here? You'll not hold your job, you won't, if you can't keep that man safe and sound. Why, he gets out every night. [*She crosses toward bedroom door*]

ATTENDANT: 'Ere, don't go, Miss.

MAID: Miss Lucy's asked for the evening paper.

[MAID *smiles as she goes off; indicates speedy return.* ATTENDANT *looks out of window and then looks under couch.*

MAID *returns. Her line comes just as* ATTENDANT *bends over, causing him to jump back, frightened*]

MAID: Well, have you found him?

ATTENDANT: No, I 'aven't. [*Confidentially*] And I'll tell you, Miss, this job is fair gettin' on my nerves.

MAID: Your nerves? And what about *my* nerves? Isn't it enough to have dogs howling every night and foreign counts bobbing up out of the floor, and Miss Lucy taking on the way she does, with everybody having their veins drained of blood for her, and this Dutch Sherlock Holmes with the X-ray eyes about, without you letting that Renfield loose?

ATTENDANT: [*Grieved*] I 'aven't let 'im loose. . . Just now I 'ears a noise like a wolf 'owling. I opens 'is door with me key, and what do I see but 'is legs goin' through the window as though 'e was goin' to climb down that smooth wall. 'E ain't 'uman, 'e ain't.

MAID: Climb down the wall?

ATTENDANT: [*Gloomily*] I don't expect no one to believe it, but I seen it, and w'ot's more, I grabbed 'old of 'is feet, I did.

MAID: [*Laughs unbelievingly*] Climbing down, head first, like a bat?

ATTENDANT: Queer your mention of bats, for just as I got 'old of 'im, a big bat flies in the window and 'its me in the face.

MAID: [*Mysteriously*] I know where that bat came from.

ATTENDANT: [*Startled*] You do? Where?

MAID: Out of your belfry. [*Crosses to head of couch and arranges pillows, then to dresser*]

ATTENDANT: No, Miss, it's Gawd's truth I'm tellin' yer . . . [*Look from her*] . . . out that bat flies, and the looney is gone, but I 'eard 'im laugh, and Gawd, what a laugh. Blimme, but I'll catch it from the Guv'ner for this.

MAID: [*At dressing table*] If you tell the Guvernor any such tales he'll shut you up with the looney.

ATTENDANT: Lor', Miss, but you're a smart one . . . that's just what I've been thinkin', and I daren't tell 'im what I see or what I 'eard. But 'e's 'armless, this bloke.

MAID: [*Ironically*] Wouldn't hurt a fly, would he?

ATTENDANT: 'Urt a fly? Oh, no, not 'e. 'E only *eats* 'em. Why, 'e'd rather eat a few blue-bottles than a pound of the best steak, and what 'e does to spiders is a crime.

MAID: It seems to me somebody will be coming after *you* in a minute, you and your spiders.

ATTENDANT: I say, Miss. This is a queer neighborhood. [*Looking out of window*] What a drop that is to the ground. [*Turns to her*] You don't have to be afraid of burglars, do you? No way of getting up here unless they fly . . . Don't you never feel a bit lonesome like, out there . . . [*Points to window*] . . . on your nights off?

MAID: Just lately I have a bit. [*Looks toward window*] I never noticed trees had such shadows before.

ATTENDANT: Well . . . if you feel you'd like a h'escort, Miss . . .

MAID: I'll not walk with you in your uniform. People might be taking me for one of your loonies.

ATTENDANT: [*Puts arm around her*] In mufti, then, tomorrow night.

MAID: I say, you haven't wasted much time, have you?

ATTENDANT: I've 'ad my eye on you.

MAID: Better keep that eye on your looney, or you'll be looking for a new job [ATTENDANT *tries to kiss her. She pushes him off and slaps him*] Here, you. Buzz off. Your Guvenor will be in any minute. [*Gestures to door*] Go find your looney.

ATTENDANT: Oh, orl right, but I've got somethin' 'ere that'll tempt 'im back to 'is room.

MAID: Why, what's that?

[*He fumbles in pocket. She comes up to him*]

ATTENDANT: [*Takes white mouse by tail out of pocket; holds it in her face*] This 'ere.

MAID: [*Screams; climbs on chair; holds skirt*] Take it away! Take it away!

ATTENDANT: [*Mouse climbs up his arm to shoulder. To mouse*] Come on, Cuthbert. We ain't too popular. [*Offended, walks off left with dignity, remarking from door:*] Some people 'ave *no* sense of humor.

SEWARD: [*Enters hastily from bedroom*] What was that?

MAID: [*Puts down her skirt*] Pardon, sir. He frightened me with that . . . that animal.

SEWARD: [*Agitated*] Animal, what animal?

MAID: A white mouse, sir.

SEWARD: [*Relieved*] You mustn't scream . . . not in this house . . . *now*.

MAID: I'm sorry, sir, but that nasty little beast . . .

SEWARD: You alarmed Miss Lucy so. She's dreadfully upset as it is by something in the paper.

MAID: Oh, do you mean about that Hampstead Horror, sir? The lady in white who gives chocolates to little children . . .

SEWARD: [*Interrupts impatiently*] Never mind that, but I will not have Miss Lucy disturbed.

[SEWARD *returns to bedroom. Dogs howl. Lights go out.* MAID *screams. Green spot comes up on* DRACULA *who stands in center of room.* MAID *screams again as she sees him*]

DRACULA: [*Soothingly*] Forgive me. My footfall is not heavy, and your rugs are soft.

MAID: It's all right, sir . . . but how did you come in?

DRACULA: [*Smiling*] The door of this room was ajar, so I did not knock. How is Miss Lucy and her nervous prostration?

MAID: I think she's better, sir.

DRACULA: Ah, good. But the strain of Miss Lucy's illness has made you also ill.

MAID: How did you know, sir? But it's only a pain in my head that runs down into the neck.

DRACULA: [*Winningly*] I can remove this pain.

MAID: I don't understand, sir.

DRACULA: Such pains yield readily to suggestion.

MAID: [*Raises arm slightly to shield herself*] Excuse me, sir, but if it's hypnotism you mean, I'd rather have the pain.

DRACULA: Ah, you think of hypnotism as an ugly waving of arms and many passes. That is not my method. [*As he speaks he gestures quietly with his left hand and she stares at him, fascinated. Placing his left thumb against her forehead, he stares straight into her eyes. She makes a feeble effort to remove his*

hand, then remains quiescent. He now speaks coldly, impera-
tively; turns her face front before speaking] What is given can
be taken away. From now on you will have no pain. And you
have no will of your own. Do you hear me?

MAID: [*Murmurs*] I hear you.

DRACULA: When you awake you will not remember what I say.
Doctor Seward ordered you today to sleep with your mistress
every night in the same bed because of her bad dreams. Is it
not so?

MAID: [*Murmurs*] Yes, Master.

DRACULA: Your mistress is threatened by horror and by death,
but I will save her. A man whose will is at cross purposes with
mine has come to this house. I will crush him. Receive your orders. You hear me?

MAID: Yes, Master.

DRACULA: Hear and obey. From now on you will carry out any
suggestion that reaches you from my brain instantly without
question. When I will you to do a thing it shall be done. My
call will reach you soon.

[*Green spot dims out slowly.* DRACULA *exits through window. Lights come on. Dogs howl outside.* MAID *looks up at
window as* VAN HELSING *enters left. She starts when door
shuts*]

VAN HELSING: [*His face is paler. He looks drawn and weak. He
carries box tied with string*] You've not left your mistress
alone?

MAID: Doctor Seward is with her, sir. [*Sways a little*]

VAN HELSING: [*Looking at her keenly*] What's wrong with you,
my girl?

MAID: Nothing, sir.

VAN HELSING: You've just had a severe shock.

MAID: It's nothing, sir. I . . . I suddenly felt queer. [*Looks toward window*] That's all. I can't remember anything.

VAN HELSING: Mr. Harker has just arrived. Ask Doctor Seward to
come here. Remain with Miss Lucy yourself.

MAID: Yes, sir. She's dreadfully upset, sir.

VAN HELSING: Upset over what?

MAID: It's in the evening paper, sir. About the Hampstead Horror. [VAN HELSING *motions* MAID *to silence*] Yes, sir.

VAN HELSING: [*Shaken*] Oh, God, she has seen it!

[MAID *goes into bedroom.* HARKER *enters left*]

HARKER: [*Worried*] Everything just the same? [VAN HELSING *nods.* HARKER *closes door*] When I leave this house even for a few hours I dread what I . . . I dread what I may find when I come back.

VAN HELSING: And well you may, my friend. [*He places box on table under mirror*]

HARKER: God must have sent you here to help us. Without you there'd be no hope. And this morning, Professor, when you opened your veins to revive Lucy again . . .

VAN HELSING: It was the least I could do . . . for my lack of foresight was responsible for this attack.

HARKER: Don't say that.

VAN HELSING: Her maid slept with her . . . and yet we found the wolfsbane thrown off the bed to the floor.

HARKER: She was so weak, so pale, the two little wounds opened fresh again . . .

VAN HELSING: [*With gesture to box*] I have prepared a stronger defense. But our main task is not defense, but attack. What have you found in London?

HARKER: A lot, but heaven knows what it means or whether it's any use.

VAN HELSING: I, too, have had news of which I can make nothing.

SEWARD: [*Enters*] Ah, John, back from town.

HARKER: Yes. [*Sits*]

VAN HELSING: We must try to piece together what we have learned today. [*Producing telegram of several sheets*] My colleague in Bucharest wires that the Dracula family has been extinct . . . for five hundred years.

SEWARD: Can the Count be an impostor?

VAN HELSING: [*Referring to telegram*] The castle he calls his own is a desolate ruin near the border. It was built, as you said,

Harker, by the terrible Voivode Dracula, who was said to have had dealings with evil spirits. He was the last of his race. But for many generations the peasants have believed the Castle Dracula inhabited by a vampire.

HARKER: Then it must be he . . .

VAN HELSING: [*Shakes head; puts telegram back in pocket*] My friends, I am bewildered.

SEWARD: But surely this confirms your suspicions. I was incredulous till I saw that creature hovering over Lucy . . .

VAN HELSING: A vampire from Transylvania cannot be in England.

SEWARD: But why?

VAN HELSING: Because, as I have told you, the vampire must rest by day in the earth in which the corpse it inhabits was buried.

HARKER: [*Rises*] In the earth.

VAN HELSING: The vampire must return to its burial place by sunrise.

HARKER: [*Excited*] I found today that Dracula arrived at the Croydon airdome in a three-engined German plane, on March sixth.

SEWARD: March the sixth? Three days before Mina first was taken ill.

HARKER: This plane had made a nonstop flight from Sekely in Transylvania. It left just after sunset. It arrived two hours before dawn. It carried only the Count and six packing cases.

VAN HELSING: Did you learn what was in those cases?

HARKER: He told the customs people he wanted to see whether Transylvania plants would grow in a foreign climate in their native soil.

VAN HELSING: Soil? What was in those boxes?

HARKER: Just plain dirt. He left in a lorry, with the six coffinlike boxes, before sunrise.

VAN HELSING: Oh, God, yes, before sunrise. The King of Vampires, my friends. [*Crosses between* SEWARD *and* HARKER] This creature is the terrible Voivode Dracula himself! In his satanic pride and contempt, he even uses his own time. For who could suspect? For five hundred years he has been fettered to his castle because he must sleep by day in his graveyard. Five centuries pass. The airplane is invented. His chance has come, for now he can cross Europe in a single night. He prepared six coffins filled with the earth in which he must rest by day. He leaves his castle after sunset. By dawn he is in London and safe in one of his cases—a great risk, but he has triumphed. He has reached London with its teeming millions, with its "opportunity," as he said . . .

SEWARD: God protect my Lucy!

HARKER: [*To* VAN HELSING, *new tone*] I saw the estate agent from whom he bought Carfax here and got the address of four old houses he has leased in different parts of London.

VAN HELSING: One of his coffin retreats is in each of those houses.

SEWARD: Two heavy boxes were delivered at Carfax the day after he took possession.

VAN HELSING: He has scattered them, for safety. If we can find all six, we can destroy him.

SEWARD: But how?

VAN HELSING: His native earth will no longer receive his unclean form if each box is sanctified with holy water.

HARKER: Then we must get at those boxes, tear them open, one by one. If we find him, then in God's name, Professor, I demand that my hand shall drive the stake into this devil's heart and send his soul to hell!

　　[SEWARD *motions no noise because of* LUCY]

VAN HELSING: Your plan is too dangerous.

SEWARD: But why? These attacks on Lucy continue. Are we to delay while my child is dying?

HARKER: No, not for a moment.

VAN HELSING: Patience, my friends. This creature is more than mortal. His cunning is the growth of the ages. How if we find five of his boxes and close them against him, and cannot find the sixth?

SEWARD: Well?

VAN HELSING: Then he will bury himself in his last refuge, where we can never find him and sleep until we are all dead.

HARKER: Then Lucy will be safe.

VAN HELSING: For her life, yes . . . but his unclean kiss has claimed her for his own. When she dies she will become as he is, a foul thing of the night. The vampire can wait. No, my friends, there is only one way to save her from him . . . to destroy him.

SEWARD: You're right, as always.

VAN HELSING: We have one great advantage . . . by day he is a coffined corpse . . . of our search by day he can know nothing, if we leave no traces.

HARKER: God, this delay!

VAN HELSING: We must make the round of his houses and find all six boxes, without his knowledge, and *then* we act.

SEWARD: But what about the caretakers or servants?

VAN HELSING: All the houses will be empty. The vampire plays a lone hand.

[*Maniacal laugh heard behind curtains of window.* SEWARD *crosses quickly to window*]

SEWARD: Renfield!

[*He grabs* RENFIELD *by arm and throws him into room.* RENFIELD *laughs cunningly*]

VAN HELSING: He's been here all the time we've been talking.

SEWARD: Did you hear what we were saying, man?

RENFIELD: Yes, I heard . . . something . . . enough . . . [*With gestures to* SEWARD *and* HARKER] Be guided by what he says. [*Points to* VAN HELSING] It is your only hope. . . . It is her only hope. [*Crosses to* VAN HELSING] It is *my* only hope. [*Falls on knees before* VAN HELSING] Save my soul! Save my soul! I am weak. You are strong. I am crazy. You are sane. You are good and he is evil.

VAN HELSING: [*Impressively*] I will save you, Renfield, but you must tell me what you know. Everything.

RENFIELD: [*Rises*] Know? What should I know? I don't know anything. [*Taps head*] You say I'm mad and Doctor Seward will tell you about that. You mustn't pay any attention to anything I say.

SEWARD: We can't waste time with this fellow. I'll have him taken away. [*Crosses to bell*]

RENFIELD: [*To* SEWARD] Fool, fool, and I thought you were wise! The whole world is mad just now, and if you want help you must come to a madman to get it. [*Little laugh, cunningly*] But I'll not give it to you, I'm afraid. [*Turns to window*] A wise madman will obey him who is strong and not the weak.

VAN HELSING: [*Moves to him fiercely*] Him? Whom do you mean?

RENFIELD: Need we mention names among friends? Come, Professor, be reasonable. What have I got to gain by being on your side? The Doctor keeps me shut up all day, and if I'm good he gives me a little sugar to spread out for my flies, but on the other hand, if I serve him . . . [*Points to window*]

VAN HELSING: [*Sharply, taking him by coat*] The blood is the life, eh, Renfield? [*Dragging him again*] What have you to do with Count Dracula?

RENFIELD: [*Convulsed with terror*] Dracula! [*Drawing himself up defiantly*] I never even heard the name before!

VAN HELSING: You are lying!

RENFIELD: Madmen, Professor, lack the power to discriminate between truth and falsehood . . . [*Breaks away*] . . . so I take no offense at what most men would consider an affront. [*Crosses to* SEWARD] Send me away! I asked you to before and you wouldn't. If you only knew what has happened since then. I dare not tell you more. I dare not! I should die in torment if I betrayed . . .

VAN HELSING: Doctor Seward will send you away if you speak.

SEWARD: Yes, Renfield. [RENFIELD *moans*] I offer you your soul in exchange for what you know.

RENFIELD: God will not damn a poor lunatic's soul. God knows the devil is too strong for us who have weak minds. But send me away . . . I want you to promise, Doctor Seward!

SEWARD: If you will speak.

RENFIELD: [*Pause. Looks at* SEWARD, VAN HELSING, HARKER, *and* SEWARD *again, then speaks as a sane man*] Then I will tell you. Count Dracula is . . . [*Bat comes in window; flies out again.* RENFIELD *rushes to window with arms outstretched, scream-*

ing] Master! Master! I didn't say anything! I told them nothing. I'm loyal to you. I am your slave.

[SEWARD *and* HARKER *rush to window*]

SEWARD: [*Looking out window*] There's a big bat flying in a cir-
cle. It's gone.
HARKER: What's that, just passing that small shrub? It looks like
a big gray dog.
VAN HELSING: Are you sure it was a dog?
HARKER: Well, it might easily be a wolf, Oh, but that's nonsense.
Our nerves are making us see things.
VAN HELSING: Come, Renfield. What were you about to say?
RENFIELD: Nothing, nothing.

[LUCY *comes in from bedroom with newspaper*]

LUCY: Professor . . . have you seen what's in this . . .
VAN HELSING: Miss Lucy, give it to . . .
RENFIELD: [*Crosses to her*] Are you Miss Seward?
LUCY: I am.

[SEWARD *moves closer to her; indicates* HARKER *to ring bell*]

RENFIELD: Then in the name of the merciful and compassionate
God, leave this place at once!

[*She turns to him.* VAN HELSING *motions silence to others*]

LUCY: But this is my home. Nothing would induce me to leave.
RENFIELD: [*Sane*] Oh, that's true. You wouldn't go if they tried
to drag you away, would you? It's too late. What a fool I am. I
shall be punished for this and it can't do any good. It's too
late. [*In tone of pity*] You are so young, so beautiful, so pure.
Even I have decent feelings sometimes, and I must tell you,
and if you don't go your soul will pay for it. You're in the
power of . . . [*Bat flies in window and out.* RENFIELD *rushes
to window and screams.* SEWARD *moves toward couch.* HARKER
crosses to LUCY *to protect her*] The Master is at hand!

[RENFIELD *crosses back on knees.* ATTENDANT *appears at
door*]

SEWARD: Butterworth!

[SEWARD *helps* RENFIELD *up, then* ATTENDANT *grasps him and takes him to door*]

RENFIELD: [*At door*] Goodbye, Miss Seward. Since you will not heed my warning, I pray God that I may never see your face again.

[*He exits with* ATTENDANT]

LUCY: What did he mean, Professor? What did he mean? Why did he say that?

[*She goes off into bedroom, in hysterics.* HARKER *follows her*]

SEWARD: That crazy thing in league with the devil; horrible, and Lucy already upset by something in the paper.

VAN HELSING: Go in and get that paper from her.

SEWARD: Whatever it is, she keeps on reading that article again and again.

VAN HELSING: Take it away from her, man, and come back to me. [*Places hand on forehead as if faint*]

SEWARD: Don't overdo it, Van Helsing. God knows where we should be if you went under. After a transfusion operation, at your age you really ought to be in bed . . . the loss of so much blood is serious.

VAN HELSING: I never felt more fit in my life.

SEWARD: I only ask you not to overestimate your strength now, when we lean on you. . . . [*As he exits*] Feeling fit, are you? Just look at yourself in the glass.

[VAN HELSING, *alone, registers as tired and exhausted, and walks slowly across room, looking at his drawn face in mirror.* DRACULA, *with stealthy tread, in evening dress and cloak as before, enters from window and walks slowly to directly behind* VAN HELSING]

VAN HELSING: [*Looking at himself, touching face, shakes head*] The devil.

DRACULA: Come. [VAN HELSING *turns suddenly to him and looks back into the mirror*] Not as bad as that. [*Suave, cold, ironical*]

VAN HELSING: [*Long look in mirror, then turns to* DRACULA. *Controlling himself with difficulty*] I did not hear you, Count.

DRACULA: I am often told that I have a light footstep.

VAN HELSING: I was looking in the mirror. Its reflection covers the whole room, but I cannot see . . .

[*Pause. He turns to mirror.* DRACULA, *face convulsed by fury, picks up small vase with flowers from stand, smashes mirror, pieces of mirror and vase tumbling to floor.* VAN HELSING *steps back; looks at* DRACULA *with loathing and terror*]

DRACULA: [*Recovering composure*] Forgive me, I dislike mirrors. They are the playthings in man's vanity. . . . And how's the fair patient?

VAN HELSING: [*Meaningly*] The diagnosis presents difficulties.

DRACULA: I feared it might, my friend.

VAN HELSING: Would you care to see what I have prescribed for my patient?

DRACULA: Anything that you prescribe for Miss Lucy has the greatest interest for me.

[VAN HELSING *crosses to table to get box.* DRACULA *crosses, meets* VAN HELSING *coming back with box.* VAN HELSING *deliberately turns away from him, goes to small table right of arch, turns front as he opens pocketknife and, in cutting string of parcel, cuts his finger. He gives slight exclamation of pain; holds up finger covered with blood.* DRACULA *starts for* VAN HELSING *with right hand raised, then keeping control with difficulty, turns away so as not to see blood.* VAN HELSING *stares at him a moment, then walks up and sticks bleeding finger in front of him*]

VAN HELSING: The prescription is a most unusual one.

[DRACULA, *baring teeth, makes sudden snap at finger.* VAN HELSING *turns away quickly; ties handkerchief around it.* DRACULA *again regains poise with an effort*]

DRACULA: The cut is not deep . . . I . . . looked.

VAN HELSING: [*Opening parcel*] No, but it will serve. Here is my medicine for Miss Lucy. [DRACULA *comes up to* VAN HELSING, *who quickly holds handful of wolfsbane up to his face.*

DRACULA *leaps back, face distorted with rage and distress. shielding himself with cloak. Putting wolfsbane back in box*] You do not care for the smell?

DRACULA: You are a wise man, Professor . . . for one who has not lived even a single lifetime.

VAN HELSING: You flatter me, Count.

DRACULA: But not wise enough to return to Holland at once, now that you have learned what you have learned.

VAN HELSING: [*Shortly*] I preferred to remain. [*Meaningly*] Even though a certain lunatic here attempted to kill me.

DRACULA: [*Smiling*] Lunatics are difficult. They do not do what they are told. They even try to betray their benefactors. But when servants fail to obey orders, the Master must carry them out for himself.

VAN HELSING: [*Grimly*] I anticipated as much.

DRACULA: [*Gazing at him intently*] In the past five hundred years, Professor, those who have crossed my path have all died, and some not pleasantly. [*Continues to gaze at* VAN HELSING; *lifts his arm slowly; says with terrible emphasis and force*] Come . . . here. [VAN HELSING *pales, staggers, then slowly takes three steps toward* DRACULA. *Very slight pause as* VAN HELSING *attempts to regain control of himself, then takes another step toward* DRACULA; *pauses, places hand to brow, then completely regains control of himself and looks away*] Ah, your will is strong. Then I must come to you. [*Advances to* VAN HELSING, *who takes out of breast pocket small velvet bag.* DRACULA *stops*] More medicine, Professor?

VAN HELSING: More effective than wolfsbane, Count.

DRACULA: Indeed? [*Starts for* VAN HELSING's *throat.* VAN HELSING *holds bag out toward him.* DRACULA's *face becomes convulsed with terror and he retreats left before* VAN HELSING, *who follows him*] Sacrilege.

VAN HELSING: [*Continuing to advance*] I have a dispensation.

[VAN HELSING *has cut him off from the door and remorselessly presses him toward window.* DRACULA, *livid with rage and snarling, backs out of the window. As* DRACULA *is*

*just outside the window he spreads his cape like a bat and
gives a long satirical laugh as he makes exit.* VAN HELSING
*almost collapses; puts bag back in pocket; crosses himself;
mops perspiration from brow with handkerchief. A shot is
heard.* VAN HELSING *leaps up; rushes to window. Bat circles
almost into his face. He staggers back.* SEWARD *hurries in,
carrying newspaper*]

SEWARD: God, Van Helsing, what was that? [*Dropping newspaper on table*]

VAN HELSING: A revolver shot. It came as a relief. That at least is
something human.

SEWARD: Who broke the mirror?

VAN HELSING: I.

[HARKER *enters*]

HARKER: Sorry if I startled you. I saw that infernal bat around
this side of the house. I couldn't resist a shot.

SEWARD: Did you hit it?

HARKER: Why, I . . .

VAN HELSING: The bullet was never made, my friend, that could
harm *that* bat. *My* weapons are stronger.

HARKER: What do you mean?

VAN HELSING: Dracula has been here.

SEWARD: Good God!

HARKER: How did he get in?

VAN HELSING: You ask how the Vampire King, during the hours
of night, the hours that are his, comes and goes? As the wind,
my friend, as he pleases. He came to kill me. . . . But I carry
a power stronger than his.

HARKER: What power?

VAN HELSING: I expected an attack. I secured a dispensation
from the Cardinal. I have with me . . . [*Crosses himself*] . . .
the Host. [HARKER *crosses himself*] He came. I proved my case
if it needed proof. The mirror does not reflect this *man that
was*, who casts no shadow. See, I cut my finger, *it* leapt at the
blood, but before the sacred wafer *it* fled.

SEWARD: Lucy must not know.

VAN HELSING: [*Gently, worried*] Miss Lucy knows . . . more than you think.

HARKER: How can she? If she knew, she'd tell me.

VAN HELSING: As these attacks continue she comes more and more under his power. There is a mystic link between them. [SEWARD *sighs*], Oh, it is hard to bear, but you must face it. It may be that he can already learn what passes in her mind. And so Miss Lucy must not be told that we know about earth boxes . . . for he may learn . . . whatever she knows.

[LUCY *enters*]

SEWARD: But Professor, that would mean that Lucy is in collusion with this creature. That's impossible. . . .

[LUCY *crosses to table; takes newspaper*]

VAN HELSING: No, no, Miss Lucy, you must not.

HARKER: Lucy, what's in this paper that's upset you?

LUCY: [*Hands newspaper to* HARKER] Read it, John.

[HARKER *takes newspaper; reads.* VAN HELSING *moves as if to stop him, then checks himself*]

VAN HELSING: No, Harker, no.

LUCY: Read it!

[LUCY *sits on couch. They all listen*]

HARKER: [*Reading*] "The Hampstead Horror. Further attacks on small children, committed after dark by a mysterious and beautiful woman in Hampstead, are reported today. Narratives of three small girls, all under ten years of age, tally in essential details. Each child speaks of a beautiful lady in white who gave her chocolates, enticed her to some secluded corner and there kissed and fondled her and bit her slightly in the throat." [*He looks at* SEWARD *and* LUCY]

LUCY: Go on.

HARKER: [*Reading*] "The wounds are trivial. The children suffered no other harm and do not seem to have been fright-

ened. Indeed, one small girl told her mother she hoped she
might see the beautiful lady again."

[*He turns to* LUCY. SEWARD *takes paper from* HARKER]

VAN HELSING: So soon . . . so soon.

[HARKER *and* SEWARD *look at each other*]

SEWARD: You know what has been happening, Lucy? [LUCY
nods]

HARKER: Professor Van Helsing knows, too, Lucy, and he knows
how to protect you.

LUCY: Is it not too late?

VAN HELSING: No, Miss Lucy, it is not too late.

SEWARD: These poor innocent children . . .

VAN HELSING: [*To* SEWARD] You think Count Dracula . . .

LUCY: [*Shudders*] Not that name.

VAN HELSING: You think the Werewolf has done this too?

SEWARD: Of course, in the form of a woman. Who else could it
be?

VAN HELSING: It is worse. Far worse.

HARKER: Worse? What do you mean?

[LUCY *is motionless, her face frozen in horror*]

VAN HELSING: Miss Lucy knows.

LUCY: The woman in white . . . is Mina.

HARKER: Mina. But she's dead, Lucy.

LUCY: She has joined . . . the Master.

SEWARD: Oh, God, have pity on us all. [*Drops newspaper on
chair*]

VAN HELSING: My dear Miss Lucy, I will not ask you how you
know. After tonight no more little children will meet the
woman in white. She will remain at rest . . . in the tomb
where you laid her. And her soul, released from this horror,
will be with God.

LUCY: How can you do this?

VAN HELSING: Don't ask me.

LUCY: [*Takes hold of* VAN HELSING'S *arm*] Professor, if you can
save Mina's soul after her death, can you save mine?

HARKER: Oh, Lucy! [*Sitting on couch, arm around her*]

VAN HELSING: [*Takes her hand*] I will save you. In God's name, I swear it. And He has given me a sign . . . in this room tonight.

LUCY: Then promise me one thing. Whatever you plan to do, whatever you know, do not tell me. [*Turns to* HARKER] Not even if I beg *you* to tell me, swear that you will not, now, while I am still yours, while I am myself, promise it.

HARKER: I promise it. [*Takes her in his arms; tries to kiss her*]

LUCY: [*Breaks from him, horrified*] No, no, John! You mustn't kiss me. Promise that you never will, not even if I beg you to.

HARKER: I promise.

VAN HELSING: My dear Miss Lucy, from tonight on one of us will be awake all night, here in this room, next to your bedroom, with your door open.

LUCY: [*Murmurs*] You are so good.

VAN HELSING: Yes, and I will make the room safe for you. Your maid will be with you. [HARKER *talks to* LUCY *on couch while* VAN HELSING *takes handful of wolfsbane*] Doctor, rub these over the window in the little room there. See, like this. [*He starts rubbing around edge of window*] Rub it around the sashes and especially above the lock. [SEWARD *watches* VAN HELSING *rubbing, then takes wolfsbane from* VAN HELSING *quickly, and goes out through arch.* VAN HELSING *turns, goes to table and takes out wreath of wolfsbane*] See, I have made this wreath that you must wear around your neck tonight. While you wear this those . . . dreams . . . cannot come to you. [*Hangs wolfsbane around her neck. Takes out of pocket crucifix on cord, which he also hangs around her neck*] Swear to me that you will not take these off.

LUCY: I promise.

VAN HELSING: Swear it on the cross.

LUCY: [*Kisses cross*] I swear it!

[VAN HELSING *crosses toward door*]

HARKER: Professor, surely the Host is more powerful than this wolfsbane.

VAN HELSING: Of course.

HARKER: Then leave the Host with her . . . nothing can harm her then.

VAN HELSING: No, the Host cannot be used where there has been pollution. [*Screams off left*] What is it?

[ATTENDANT *enters left.* MAID *comes in from bedroom;* SEWARD *enters from arch*]

ATTENDANT: It's Renfield, sir.

SEWARD: Why haven't you got him locked up?

ATTENDANT: Because he's barred himself in, sir. He got hold of one of the patients. He had her by the throat.

[*He exits.* LUCY *rises*]

VAN HELSING: Ah . . . human blood now! [*Starting*] Come, Seward! Come, Harker!

SEWARD: I should have had him sent away!

[MAID *comes to* LUCY. VAN HELSING *and* SEWARD *exit.* HARKER *hesitates, then follows them off.* HARKER *ad libs during exit,* "It's all right, Lucy. I'll be right back," *etc.*]

LUCY: John . . . [*To* MAID] Don't you leave me, too.

MAID: Of course I won't, Miss Lucy. It's nothing but a quarrel among the patients. Mr. Harker will be back soon. [MAID *places her on couch.* LUCY *swoons.* MAID *gets smelling salts*] Here, Miss Lucy. [DRACULA'S *face appears back of tapestry on rear wall; disappears after a count of eight or nine.* MAID *steps down right, gets message, then returns. Puts salts back on dresser, crosses to* LUCY] The evil-smelling flowers have made you faint. [*Takes crucifix and wreath from around* LUCY'S *neck, throws them on floor; crosses two steps down right. Another message comes to her. Puts hand to head, turns slowly, looks at window, steps toward couch*] It is so close, Madam. A little air . . . [*Turns to window.* LUCY *moans again.* MAID *pulls back latch; opens window. As window opens, clouds of mist roll in. Steps down. Gets message. Count eight. Switches out lights, then exits into bedroom. The stage is now dark. Dogs without far and near, howl in terror. A gauze curtain comes down and a green light dims up covering the couch and center of the stage, revealing* DRACULA *standing center with back to audience, hands outstretched to resemble a large bat. As he moves up a few steps,* LUCY *slowly rises from couch and falls into his arms. A long kiss and then, as she falls back on his right arm, he bares her throat and starts to bite her as:*

CURTAIN

ACT THREE

The library. Thirty-two hours later, shortly before sunrise.

A stake and hammer are on desk. Dogs howl. Curtains move as if someone is entering window. Then chair back of desk, which is turned upstage, moves around, facing front. After a moment, VAN HELSING *enters with* SEWARD. VAN HELSING *paces up and down;* SEWARD *sits at desk. The center doors are flung open and the* ATTENDANT *comes in.*

VAN HELSING: What is it?

ATTENDANT: [*To* VAN HELSING] Anybody w'ot wants my job, sir, can 'ave it.

[SEWARD *rouses himself*]

SEWARD: What's the matter?

ATTENDANT: I knows what I knows, and w'ot I seen I saw, and I 'ops it by the first train, and don't ask for no wages in loo of notice.

VAN HELSING: Where's Renfield?

ATTENDANT: If you asks me, I says 'e's probably payin' a little visit to 'ell.

SEWARD: You've let him escape again?

ATTENDANT: Look 'ere, sir. 'avin', so to speak, resigned, I don't 'ave to put up with any more from any of you. [*Looks at* VAN

HELSING *and* SEWARD] W'ot a man can't 'elp, 'e can't 'elp, and that's that.

[SEWARD *sinks back on desk, head in hands*]

VAN HELSING: Can't you see, man, that Doctor Seward is not well? Will you desert him when he needs all the help he can get?

ATTENDANT: Puttin' it that way, sir, I ain't the man to run under fire. But I'm sick and tired of being told off for what ain't my fault.

VAN HELSING: We don't blame you. No bolts or bars could hold Renfield.

ATTENDANT: [SEWARD *looks up at him*] Now, sir, you're talkin' sense. I 'ad 'im in a straightjacket this time. Nearly all yesterday I worked at clampin' bars across the winder. Now I finds them bars pulled apart like they was made o' cheese and 'im gone.

VAN HELSING: Then try to find him.

ATTENDANT: Find 'im, sir? Find 'im? I can't chase him up and down the wall. I ain't no bloody mountain goat! [*Exits*]

VAN HELSING: The Thing mocks us. A few hours after he finds out what we know, and what we have done, he comes here, and drags that poor creature of his to himself.

SEWARD: [*In dull, hopeless tone*] What can the vampire want with Renfield?

VAN HELSING: Renfield is serving an apprenticeship . . . to join the Vampire King after his death. We must prevent that.

SEWARD: What does Renfield matter? . . . If we are beaten, then there is no God.

VAN HELSING: [*Crosses to him*] We dare not despair, Seward.

SEWARD: To figure out in advance what anyone would do who got on his track!

VAN HELSING: I thought we had him when we broke into Carfax and found two earth boxes there and then found one box in each of his four other houses, and when I pried up the lid on the sixth box I was sure we would find him there, helpless.

SEWARD: [*Bitterly*] Empty.

VAN HELSING: An empty packing case, left as a blind.

SEWARD: He only brought six in his plane, so there can be only the one left.

VAN HELSING: Only one, but hidden where we can never find it. And now we've put him on his guard.

SEWARD: Yes. [*Chair turns back. Curtains flap out.* SEWARD *looks at wrist watch*] It's not half an hour till sunrise. [*Rises and crossing to fireplace*] Poor John has been sitting up with Lucy for nine hours. She'll be safe at dawn and he can get some sleep . . . if anyone can sleep in this house.

VAN HELSING: Whoever else sleeps or does not sleep, Miss Lucy will sleep at dawn.

SEWARD: Another horror?

VAN HELSING: Oh, you've noticed how she keeps awake all night now and sleeps by day.

SEWARD: Is that part of . . . the change?

VAN HELSING: Of course. And sometimes . . . the look that comes into her face.

SEWARD: [*Turns face away in horror*] Don't, man, for God's sake, I can't bear it!

VAN HELSING: We must face the facts, for her sake.

SEWARD: How could it have got at her with the wolfsbane and the cross around her neck? [*Pause*] Suggestion, conveyed from the Monster?

VAN HELSING: Yes. He must have impelled the maid to take away the wolfsbane and cross and open the window. I should have foreseen that.

SEWARD: Don't blame yourself. The devil is more cunning than we are. [*Sits couch*] Yet Lucy seems better. Until this last attack she's always been exhausted, but at sunset last night, when she woke up after sleeping all day . . .

VAN HELSING: There was blood in her cheeks again.

SEWARD: Yes, thank God.

VAN HELSING: [*With terrible emphasis*] My poor friend, *where does that blood come from?*

SEWARD: What do you suggest now? What fresh horror . . .

[*Door left opens a crack. Long skinny hand protrudes into room.* SEWARD *sees it first and starts in alarm. Rises.* VAN

HELSING *turns quickly. Door opens slowly and* RENFIELD
slinks in]

RENFIELD: Is not half past five in the morning a strange hour for
men who aren't crazy to be up and about? [*Crosses to window*]

VAN HELSING: [*Aside to* SEWARD] We may get help from this
thing that's still half-human. [*To* RENFIELD] Renfield.

RENFIELD: [*Crosses, with growing hysteria*] He's after me! He's
going to kill me!

VAN HELSING: Help us, Renfield, and we'll save you.

RENFIELD: You, you poor puny man, you measure your brains
against his? You don't know what you're dealing with! You, a
thickheaded Dutchman and a fool of an alienist, and a young
cub of a boy. Why, not all the soldiers and police in London
could stop the Master from doing as he likes.

VAN HELSING: But God can stop him!

RENFIELD: God permits evil. Why does He permit evil if He is
good? Tell me that.

SEWARD: How did you escape through those iron bars?

RENFIELD: [*Cunningly*] Madmen have a great strength, Doctor.

VAN HELSING: Come, Renfield, we know you didn't wrench those
bars apart yourself.

RENFIELD: [*Sane*] No, I didn't. I wanted them there. I hoped
they'd keep him out. He did it, then he called to me and I had
to come. [*Back to insanity*] The Master is angry. He promised
me eternal life and live things, live things, big ones, not flies
and spiders; and blood to drink, always blood. I must obey
him but I don't want to be like him. . . . I am mad, I know,
and bad, too, for I've taken lives, but they were only little
lives. I'm not like him. I wouldn't like a human life. [LUCY
laughs offstage and says, "Oh, John!" as she enters with
HARKER. LUCY *has changed; there is blood in her cheeks, she is
stronger and seems full of vitality. She and* HARKER *stop in
surprise at seeing* RENFIELD. *To* LUCY] And why did I seek to
betray him? For you. [*She smiles*] I said I'd serve the devil,
but I didn't serve him honestly. I don't like women with no
blood in them. [LUCY *laughs*] And yet I warned you and made

him angry, and now . . . [*Working into frenzy*] . . . perhaps
he will kill me. [LUCY *laughs*] And I won't get any more live
things to eat. There'll be no more blood.

> [RENFIELD *starts for* LUCY's *throat.* HARKER *grasps him by
> right arm,* VAN HELSING *by left arm, then* SEWARD *steps in
> and takes* HARKER's *place as* RENFIELD *struggles violently.*
> SEWARD *and* VAN HELSING *bear him away, struggling and
> screaming*]

HARKER: Lucy, darling, you mustn't mind that poor, crazed creature.

LUCY: [*With low laugh as before*] I don't. He amuses me.

> [*She crosses to divan and sits*]

HARKER: Oh, Lucy, how can you? The poor devil! Thank God
. . . it will soon be dawn now.

LUCY: Dawn. The ebb tide of life. I hate the dawn. How can
people like daylight? At night I am really alive. The night was
made to enjoy life, and love. . . . [HARKER *turns to her; hesitates*] Come to me, John, my own John.

> [*He comes and sits next to her*]

HARKER: Lucy, I'm so happy that you are better and strong
again. . . .

LUCY: I've never been so well . . . so full of vitality. I was only a
poor, washed-out, pale creature. I don't know what made you
love me, John. There was no reason why you should. But there
is *now*.

HARKER: I worship you.

LUCY: Then tell me something, John. [HARKER *turns slightly
away*] If you love me, you'll tell me. . . . Now don't turn
away from me again.

HARKER: [*Wearily and sadly*] You made me promise that I
wouldn't tell you . . . anything.

LUCY: Oh, but I release you from your promise. There, now.
What were you and Father and the funny Professor doing all
day?

HARKER: I can't tell you. I promised.

LUCY: [*Angrily*] You say you love me, but you don't trust me.

HARKER: I would trust you with my life, my soul.

LUCY: Then prove it. What were you doing . . . over there in Carfax? With the hammer and the horrible iron stake. [*He shakes his head. She registers anger. He puts his head in his hands, as though crying*] You don't think I'm asking you because . . . I'm just trying to find out whether you really love me. [HARKER *recoils from her, facing up*] So you try to hide your schemes and your plots. Afraid I'd give them away, are you? You fools. Whatever *he* wants to know, he finds out for himself. He knows what you do. He knows what you think. He knows everything.

HARKER: Lucy!

[*He puts his head in her lap and sobs.* LUCY *makes clawlike movement with both her hands, then as he sobs she changes attitude and gently strokes his head*]

LUCY: My dear, I'm sorry. Let me kiss away the tears.

[*She starts to kiss him. He quickly rises; backs away a few steps*]

HARKER: No, you mustn't kiss me! You made me promise not to let you kiss me.

LUCY: You don't know why I said that, John darling. It was because I love you so much. I was afraid of what might happen. You've always thought me cold, but I've blood in my veins, hot blood, my John. And I knew if I were to kiss you . . . but I'm not afraid now. Come, will you make me say it?

HARKER: Lucy, I don't understand you.

LUCY: [*Moves toward him*] I love you. I want you. [*Stretches out her arms to him*] Come to me, my darling. I want you.

HARKER: [*Goes to her, his resistance overcome, carried away by her ardor*] Lucy, Lucy!

[*He seizes her in his arms. Slowly she takes his head and bends it back. Slowly, triumphantly she bends her head down; her mouth hovers over his. Dogs howl outside. She bends his head further back quickly. Her mouth seeks his throat. Doors center open.* VAN HELSING *rushes in, holding crucifix*]

VAN HELSING: Harker! Harker! save yourself! [*Harker rises, draws away. With outstretched arm,* VAN HELSING *holds crucifix between them.* LUCY's *face becomes convulsed with loathing and rage. She snarls like an animal, retreats, fainting onto divan.* VAN HELSING *follows, holds crucifix to her, strokes her forehead with left hand*] I warned you, my poor friend. [*He kneels beside* LUCY; *begins to chafe her temples. She revives slowly, looks about her, sees cross and seizes it and kisses it passionately.* VAN HELSING, *fervently:*] Thank God! Thank God!

[*Pause.* HARKER *crosses to divan*]

LUCY: [*Broken-hearted*] Don't come to me, John. I am unclean.

HARKER: [*Sits beside her*] My darling, in my eyes you are purity itself.

VAN HELSING: You love her, and in love there is truth. She is pure, and the evil thing that has entered her shall be rooted out.

LUCY: [*In weak voice as in previous acts; to* VAN HELSING] You said you could save Mina's soul.

VAN HELSING: Mina's soul is in heaven.

LUCY: [*Murmurs*] Tell me how.

[SEWARD *enters, comes up to group in alarm, but* VAN HELSING *motions silence*]

VAN HELSING: It is your right to know . . . now. I entered her tomb. I pried open the coffin. I found her there, sleeping, but not dead . . . not truly dead. There was blood in her cheeks, a drop of blood like a red ruby on the corner of her mouth. With a stake and hammer I struck to the heart. One scream, a convulsion, and then . . . the look of peace that came to her face when, with God's help, I had made her truly dead.

LUCY: If I die, swear to me that you will do this to my body.

VAN HELSING: It shall be done.

HARKER: I swear it.

SEWARD: And I.

LUCY: My lover, my father, my dear friend, you have sworn to save my soul. And now I am done with life. I cannot live on to become . . . what you know.

VAN HELSING: No, no, Miss Lucy, by all you hold sacred, you must not even think of suicide. That would put you in his power forever.

LUCY: I cannot face this horror that I am becoming.

HARKER: [*Rises*] We will find this *Thing* that has fouled your life, destroy him and send his soul to burning hell, and it shall be by *my* hand.

LUCY: You must destroy him if you can, but with pity in your hearts, not rage and vengeance. That poor soul who has done so much evil needs our prayers more than any other. . . .

HARKER: No, you cannot ask me to forgive.

LUCY: Perhaps I, too, will need your prayers and your pity.

VAN HELSING: My dear Miss Lucy, now, while you are yourself, help me. [*Takes her hand*]

LUCY: How can I help you? Don't tell me, no, you mustn't tell me anything.

VAN HELSING: Each time the white face, the red eyes came you were pale, exhausted afterwards. But that last time . . .

LUCY: [*Shudders*] Last time he came he said I was his bride, he would seal me to him for the centuries to come.

VAN HELSING: And then?

LUCY: And then . . . [*Rises; crosses toward door*] No, no, I can't tell you. I can't. . . .

VAN HELSING: But you must.

SEWARD: You must, Lucy!

LUCY: He scratched open one of his veins. He pressed my mouth down to it. He called it a mystic sacrament . . . he made me . . . he made me drink. . . . I can't, I can't . . . go on. . . . [*LUCY rushes off hysterically.* SEWARD *follows her*]

VAN HELSING: I warned you, my poor friend. I broke in when I heard the dogs howling.

HARKER: The dogs. Then the Werewolf is about.

VAN HELSING: He is pursuing Renfield.

HARKER: God, we must do something!

VAN HELSING: And at once. I shall leave Renfield here, as I did Miss Lucy. If the *Thing* appears, we three will bar the two doors and the window.

HARKER: [*Crosses up toward window. Laughs bitterly*] Bar? Against *that?*

VAN HELSING: Even against *that,* for we shall each carry the sacred element.

HARKER: And then?

VAN HELSING: Then I do not know. It will be terrible, for we do not know his full powers. But this I know. . . . [*Looks at watch*] It is eight minutes to sunrise. The power of all evil things ceases with the coming of day. His one last earth box is his only refuge. If we can keep him here till daybreak he must collapse. And the stake and the hammer are ready. [*Dogs howl.* HARKER *crosses to window, goes out*] He is here. Quickly! [VAN HELSING *runs to window. Seizes* RENFIELD]

RENFIELD: [*As he is dragged in by* VAN HELSING] No, no!

VAN HELSING: But you must, man, and this may save your soul and your life as well.

RENFIELD: No, no, no, not alone! Don't leave me alone! [VAN HELSING *shoves him forward.* RENFIELD *falls.* VAN HELSING *hurries out, closing door and putting lights out.* RENFIELD *slowly rises; looks about him.* RENFIELD *howls in terror; crouches in firelight as far away as possible from doors and window.* DRACULA *appears, door center, in pale blue light, in evening clothes, dress and cloak as before. Red light from fireplace covers* DRACULA. *As* DRACULA *moves,* RENFIELD's *back is to audience*] Master! I didn't do it! I said nothing. I am your slave, your dog! [DRACULA *steps toward him*] Master, don't kill me! For the love of God, let me live. Punish me . . . torture me . . . I deserve it . . . but let me live! I can't face God with all those lives on my conscience, all that blood on my hands.

DRACULA: [*With deadly calm*] Did I not promise you that you should come to me at your death, and enjoy centuries of life and power over the bodies and souls of others?

RENFIELD: Yes, Master, I want lives, I want blood . . . but I didn't want human life.

DRACULA: You betrayed me. You sought to warn my destined bride against me.

RENFIELD: Mercy, mercy, mercy, don't kill me!

[DRACULA *raises right arm very slowly toward* RENFIELD, *who screams, this time in physical pain.* RENFIELD, *like a bird before a snake, drags himself to* DRACULA, *who stands motionless. As* RENFIELD *reaches* DRACULA's *feet,* DRACULA, *with swift motion, stoops, seizes him by the throat, lifts him up, his grip stifling* RENFIELD's *screams. Doors center are thrown open.* VAN HELSING *switches on lights.* DRACULA *drops* RENFIELD, *who falls into corner below couch and remains there during following scene.* DRACULA *starts toward* VAN HELSING, *who takes case containing Host out of inside breast pocket and holds it out toward* DRACULA *in his clenched right fist.* DRACULA *recoils; turns quickly to window.* HARKER *appears through window and holds crucifix toward* DRACULA *in clenched fist.* DRACULA *recoils.* SEWARD *enters window, holding crucifix. The three men stand during the following scene with right arms pointing toward* DRACULA. *He turns, walks to fireplace, turns and faces them*]

DRACULA: [*Ironically*] My friends, I regret I was not present to receive your calls at my house.

VAN HELSING: [*Looks at watch*] Four minutes until sunrise.

DRACULA: [*Looking at wrist watch*] Your watch is correct, Professor.

VAN HELSING: Your life in death has reached its end.

SEWARD: By God's mercy.

DRACULA: [HARKER *steps toward* DRACULA. DRACULA, *turning to them, suavely*] Its end? Not yet, Professor. I have still more than three minutes to add to my five hundred years.

HARKER: And three minutes from now you'll be in hell, where a thousand years of agony will not bring you one second nearer the end of your punishment.

VAN HELSING: Silence, Harker. Miss Lucy forbade this. She asked for prayer, and for pity. [*To* DRACULA] Make your peace with God, Man-That-Was. We are not your judges . . . we know not how this curse my have come upon you.

DRACULA: [*Furiously*] You fools! You think with your wafers, your wolfsbane, you can destroy me . . . me, the king of my kind? You shall see. Five of my earth boxes you have polluted. Have you found the sixth?

VAN HELSING: You cannot reach your sixth refuge now. Take your true form as Werewolf if you will. Your fangs may rend us, but we have each sworn to keep you here . . . [*Looks at watch*] . . . for two minutes and a half, when you must collapse and we can make an end.

DRACULA: *You* keep *me*. Fools, listen and let my words ring in your ears all your lives, and torture you on your deathbeds! I go, I go to sleep in my box for a hundred years. You have accomplished that much against me, Van Helsing. But in a century I shall wake, and call my bride to my side from her tomb, my Lucy, my Queen. [HARKER *and* SEWARD *move closer*] I have other brides of old times who await me in their vaults in Transylvania. But I shall set *her* above them all.

HARKER: Should you escape, we know how to save Lucy's soul, if not her life.

DRACULA: [*Moving left*] Ah, the stake. Yes, but only if she dies by day. I shall see that she dies by night. She shall come to an earth box of mine at her death and await her Master. To do to her what you did to my Mina, Van Helsing, you must find her body, and that you will not.

HARKER: Then she shall die by day.

DRACULA: You will kill her? You lack the courage, you poor rat of flesh and blood!

SEWARD: Silence, John . . . he is doomed. This is his revenge. He hopes to trouble us . . . afterwards.

VAN HELSING: [*Looks at watch*] Thirty seconds.

[*They move in*]

DRACULA: [*Calmy, suavely again*] I thank you for reminding me of the time.

VAN HELSING: Harker, open the curtains. [HARKER *opens curtains. Red light of approaching dawn outside*] That is the East. The sun will rise beyond the meadow there.

[DRACULA *pulls cape over his head*]

SEWARD: [*Glancing behind, leaves wolfsbane on desk as he looks up at window*] The clouds are coloring.

HARKER: God's daybreak.

[HARKER *leaves crucifix on desk.* VAN HELSING *checks watch.* SEWARD *and* HARKER *step in*]

DRACULA: [*Coolly. Turns upstage, with back to them*] A pleasant task you have set yourself, Mr. Harker.

VAN HELSING: Ten seconds. Be ready when he collapses.

[SEWARD *crosses to hold* DRACULA's *cape on left of* DRACULA. HARKER *holds cape on right of* DRACULA]

HARKER: *The sun!* The stake, Professor . . . the stake! Hold him, Doctor.

SEWARD: I've got him.

[DRACULA, *with loud burst of mocking laughter, vanishes on the word "sun," leaving the two men holding the empty cape. A flash goes off in front of fireplace.* HARKER *backs down left, drops empty cape in front of desk. The three men look around them*]

HARKER: Up the chimney, as a bat. You heard what he said?

SEWARD: God will not permit it. What's to be done now, Van Helsing?

VAN HELSING [*Crosses, after looking at the prostrate* RENFIELD; *motions* HARKER *and* SEWARD *to him. Whispers to them*] We'll trick Renfield into showing us! [*Then:*] Dare we leave Renfield on earth to become the slave when he dies?

SEWARD: But he's human. We can't do murder?

HARKER: I'll do it if you won't, Doctor!

VAN HELSING: [*To* SEWARD] Go to your office and get some painless drug.

RENFIELD: [*Sensing their drift without hearing their words, has been edging toward panel. Looks around room, then at panel*] They're going to kill me, Master! Save me! I am coming to you.

[*Panel in bookcase opens,* RENFIELD *exits and panel closes*]

VAN HELSING: He has shown us the way! Where does that passage go?

SEWARD: I never knew there was a passage.

[HARKER *hastens to desk; gets stake and hammer. They rush to panel*]

VAN HELSING: Only that devil has the combination. We'll break through somehow. Harker . . . quick, the hammer.

BLACKOUT

CURTAIN

SCENE 2

A vault.

Absolute darkness. Coffin right center and back of gauze drop. Flash of electric torch seen coming slowly downstairs center. Coffin contains body of DRACULA.

VAN HELSING'S VOICE: For God's sake, be careful, Seward.
SEWARD'S VOICE: These stairs go down forever.
VAN HELSING'S VOICE: May God protect us.
SEWARD'S VOICE: Is Harker there?
VAN HELSING'S VOICE: He's gone for a lantern.
SEWARD'S VOICE: I've got to the bottom.
VAN HELSING'S VOICE: Be careful. I'm right behind you.

[*Torch flashes around vault and they walk about slowly*]

SEWARD'S VOICE: What can this place be?
VAN HELSING'S VOICE: It seems an old vault. [*Stifled scream from* SEWARD. *Torch out. The torch is seen to jerk back*] What is it? Oh, where are you, man?
SEWARD'S VOICE: Sorry. I'm all right. A big rat ran across my foot.

[*Light seen coming downstairs.* HARKER *appears carrying lighted lantern which reaches floor; partially illuminates bare vault. He has stake and hammer in left hand*]

HARKER: Where are you? What is this place?
VAN HELSING: We can't see.

[HARKER *moves with lantern*]

HARKER: The place smells horribly of bats.
VAN HELSING: It has an animal smell, like the lair of a wolf.
HARKER: That's what it is.
SEWARD: [*Still flashing torch about*] There's absolutely nothing here.
HARKER: [*At extreme left with lantern*] Here's another passage.
VAN HELSING: [*Moving left*] I thought so. That must lead to Carfax. The sixth earth box is hidden somewhere here.

HARKER: And the monster is in it.

SEWARD: You can't be sure. [*As he speaks, light from his torch falls on* RENFIELD, *stretched on floor.* RENFIELD *screams as light falls on him; scurries off right into darkness*] Renfield!

[HARKER *and* VAN HELSING *hurry across*]

VAN HELSING: Where is he?

SEWARD: Over there somewhere. Even if Renfield knew about this place, that doesn't prove the vampire's here.

VAN HELSING: [*As* SEWARD *is speaking* VAN HELSING *moves right; seizes* RENFIELD] It is the vampire's life or yours! [*Drags* RENFIELD *into light of lantern*] Look at him, man, look at him. He knows.

RENFIELD: I know nothing. Let me go! Let me go, I say! [*Breaks away; goes right*]

VAN HELSING: He was stretched out here, but he wouldn't let me drag him back. Ah, Here it is. Quick, that stake.

[HARKER *and* VAN HELSING, *with stake, pry up stone slab and open coffin. The three men gaze in horror and triumph at coffin*]

SEWARD: What a horrible undead thing he is lying there!

HARKER: Let me drive it in deep!

[VAN HELSING *takes stake from* HARKER, *lowers it into the coffin.* RENFIELD *stands at right end of coffin*]

VAN HELSING: [*Almost in a whisper*] That's over the heart, Doctor?

SEWARD: [*Back of coffin*] Yes. [VAN HELSING *hands hammer to* HARKER. HARKER *raises hammer high over head; pounds stake with full force. Low groan. Silence. Stake remains fixed in* DRACULA's *body.*]

VAN HELSING: See his face now . . . the look of peace.

SEWARD: He is crumbling away.

RENFIELD: Thank God, we're free!

LUCY: [*Comes down stairway and halts at bottom*] Father, Father, John!

HARKER: Lucy!

VAN HELSING: [*Takes handful of dust; scatters it over the body*] Dust to dust . . . ashes to ashes . . .

CURTAIN

[*The curtain rises again and the entire cast comes down-stage before a black drop for curtain speech*]

VAN HELSING: [*To* AUDIENCE] Just a moment, Ladies and Gentlemen! Just a word before you go. We hope the memories of Dracula and Renfield won't give you bad dreams, so just a word of reassurance. When you get home tonight and the lights have been turned out and you are afraid to look behind the curtains and you dread to see a face appear at the window . . . why, just pull yourself together and remember that after all *there are such things.*

THE CURTAIN FALLS